Nations Within

Mary Jackson Jones,
Jena Band of Choctaw
Indians

Nations Within

THE FOUR SOVEREIGN TRIBES OF LOUISIANA

Photographs by **Tim Mueller**

Text by **Sarah Sue Goldsmith** *with* **Risa Mueller**

Louisiana State University · *Baton Rouge*

To Matthew and Nicholas

Copyright © 2003 by Louisiana State University Press
All rights reserved
Manufactured in China
First printing

12   11   10   09   08   07   06   05   04   03
5   4   3   2   1

Designer: Amanda McDonald Scallan
Typeface: Galliard
Printer and binder: Everbest Printing Co. through Four Colour Imports, Ltd.,
   Louisville, Kentucky

Library of Congress Cataloging-in-Publication Data:
Goldsmith, Sarah Sue.
   Nations within : the four sovereign tribes of Louisiana / photographs by Timothy Mueller ;
text by Sarah Sue Goldsmith with Risa Mueller.
      p. cm.
   ISBN 0-8071-2886-4 (cloth : alk. paper)
   1. Indians of North America—Louisiana—History. 2. Indians of North
America—Louisiana—Government relations. 3. Indians of North America—Louisiana—Social
life and customs. I. Mueller, Risa, 1967– II. Mueller, Timothy, 1959– III. Title.
   E78.L8G65 2003
   976.3004'97—dc21

                                             2003001610

Contents

In memory of Sarah Sue Goldsmith

Acknowledgments

This project could not have been carried out without the assistance of the Chitimacha, Tunica-Biloxi, Coushatta, and Jena Band of Choctaw tribes. The tribal members who were interviewed and photographed generously shared their lives with us, and we are sincerely grateful.

In addition, I would like to extend my heartfelt thanks to Kimberly Walden and the Cultural Department of the Chitimacha Tribe of Louisiana; Earl Barbry, Jr., of the Tunica-Biloxi Tribe of Louisiana; Leland Thompson and Rayne Langley of the Coushatta Tribe of Louisiana, and Christine Norris of the Jena Band of Choctaw Indians. I am also grateful to the leaders of each tribe for allowing us access to so many tribal members and so much tribal information: Chitimacha chairman Alton D. LeBlanc, Jr.; Coushatta chairman Lovelin Poncho; Tunica-Biloxi chairman Earl Barbry; and Jena Band of Choctaw chief B. Cheryl Smith. The administrative staff of each tribe were extremely helpful as well.

Special thanks go to friends and family, especially Werlin Robert and Travis Spradling.

I also thank the management of the Baton Rouge *Advocate*, especially Michael Hults, for allowing me the time to work on this project. Graphic designer John Gipson also deserves thanks for his skillful creation of the maps in the introduction.

Sarah Sue Goldsmith believed in this endeavor, and without her commitment we would never have taken the first steps. After fighting cancer, she passed away in the midst of the project. Her enthusiasm and compassion were sorely missed.

After much behind-the-scenes support, my wife, Risa, took on the task of helping to finish the book. For that, I am eternally grateful. Without her patience and talent this book would never have been completed.

TIM MUELLER

In 1500 B.C., the Poverty Point site in northeastern Louisiana had the largest and most elaborate earthworks in the Western Hemisphere.

Introduction

LOUISIANA is not often thought of as Indian country. Louisiana is Mardi Gras, moss-draped trees, and the birthplace of jazz. Indian country is in the open spaces out west. Among Louisiana's culturally diverse residents, however, are 27,000 people who identify themselves as Native Americans. They do not fit the stereotypes of Indians formed by the cowboy films that fed a generation's mind-set. They are oil rig workers, administrators, pharmacists, truck drivers, and wildlife agents who may be encountered in everyday life.

The native people of Louisiana may be easily overlooked because they represent less than 1 percent of the state's population. Further west in Oklahoma the number is ten times higher. After the Louisiana Purchase in 1803, even the United States government considered most area tribes insignificant, a perception reflected in Indian agent John Sibley's report of 1806. Yet four tribes in Louisiana somehow survived over the next two centuries to be recognized as sovereign nations. Today most are economic forces in their own right, and they all take pride in preserving their cultural heritage.

The history and heritage of Native Americans is rich in Louisiana. Since at least 4000 B.C., this area has been Indian country. Some of the oldest and best-preserved Indian mounds in the world can be found here, including the largest mound, Poverty Point, built around 1500 B.C. Archaeologists have identified more than seven hundred mound sites in the state, including mounds on the campus of Louisiana State University that predate Egyptian pyramids.

Hernando de Soto's expeditions of 1539 provide us with the earliest recorded history of Native Americans in the southeastern portion of what is now the United States. With his arrival on this continent, the stage was set for centuries of turmoil for native people. He often introduced himself with torture, slavery, or death, and he unwittingly left the calling card of alien diseases like smallpox and measles. The Spanish explorer found cities and towns populated by different na-

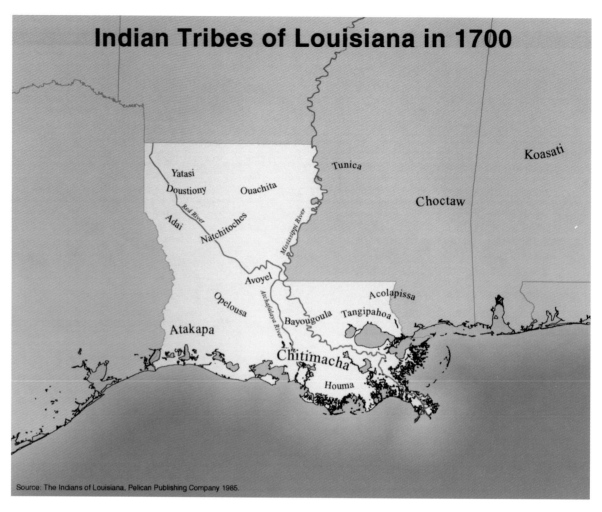

Indian Tribes of Louisiana in 1700

Koasati

Tunica

Choctaw

Yatasi
Doustiony
Ouachita
Adai
Red River
Natchitoches
Mississippi River

Avoyel

Acolapissa

Opelousa
Atchafalaya River
Bayougoula
Tangipahoa

Atakapa

Chitimacha

Houma

Source: The Indians of Louisiana, Pelican Publishing Company 1985.

tions speaking different languages. Among them was the fabled town of Quizquiz on the Mississippi River, home of the ancestors of the Tunica-Biloxi tribe, which de Soto encountered in 1541.

Altogether, Europeans encountered and dealt with the six to nine million native people on this continent as distinct, militarily powerful nations and signed treaties accordingly. The U.S. government at first recognized the different nations as inherently sovereign entities that managed their own affairs, making agreements with the native nations to acquire land for settlers.

As the new nation grew westward, treaties would be disregarded and federal policies would vacillate from the extremes of assimilation to self-determination. Federal officials forcibly removed thousands of native people from their land in the 1830s and established reservations. But by 1871 the government began encouraging Native Americans to move from reservations and become assimilated. This decimated the native population even further, and by 1900 a mere 500,000 remained.

In the early 1930s things looked more hopeful for Native Americans, as the Indian Reorganization Act encouraged economic development and the revival of indigenous cultures. But this era was quickly followed by a contradictory policy of termination, designed to force rapid assimilation. Only since 1961 has federal policy focused on the principle of self-determination, as a result of court decisions that Indian nations are sovereign entities that possess the right to rule themselves.

Along with continually changing policies came deeply rooted discrimination that native people are only now overcoming. Barred from schools, they fought their way up into an educated society. While a high percentage of native men served America proudly in the military, it wasn't until 1924 that Congress made them American citizens. In 1868, the Fourteenth Amendment to the Constitution gave blacks the right to vote but specifically excluded Native Americans. Native people were not assured the right to vote until 1965.

To survive, Native Americans either assimilated into the mainstream culture or withdrew to isolated rural areas where they could preserve their cultural identity. The irony is that though the government tried repeatedly to abolish Native American cultural heritage, it is the preservation of that very heritage that has enabled tribes to receive federal recognition. To be recognized as a sovereign nation, a tribe must meet certain criteria. It must show that it has existed as a distinct community with its own culture and an unbroken line of leadership. It must produce documents tracing genealogy to a historic tribe, and it must be able to trace the geographical locations of the tribe. In 2002, there were 561 federally recognized tribes across the United States.

Three-hundred-year-old Tunica pottery made near the time of the arrival of Europeans.

In Louisiana only four tribes have been able to overcome discrimination and changing government policies to remain intact as sovereign nations. When the first French explorers journeyed into what is now Louisiana in the early 1700s, they met many more nations. They found the Acolapissa, Adai, Atakapa, Avoyel, Bayougoula, Chitimacha, Doustiony, Houma, Natchitoches, Opelousa, Ouachita, Tangipahoa, Tensas, and Yatasi people. The tribes' names are still spread throughout the state's landscape. Indian words like Atchafalaya, Calcasieu, Catahoula and Tchefuncte are sprinkled generously on Louisiana maps, serving as names for parishes, towns and rivers. Even the word bayou is derived from the Choctaw *bayuk*.

But for many of these tribes, their names are all that remain. In a short three hundred years, most are extinct or have blended into other tribes. That some tribes remain today is amazing, revealing a remarkable resilience. The Chitimacha, who have always lived in south Louisiana, are joined on the short list of federally recognized tribes by three tribes that migrated into this area after 1700. Much like the Acadians, these three refugee tribes traveled here in search of a safer place to live. Driven by disease and warfare, the Tunica-Biloxi tribe ended its journey in Marksville in the 1770s. The Coushatta were displaced from Alabama and Georgia and wandered through Louisiana in the early 1800s before finally settling in the Elton/Kinder area in 1861. The Jena band of Choctaw found a home here in the 1830s after being forced to leave lands east of the Mississippi River.

Several other tribes in Louisiana have been trying to establish their right to be called sovereign nations. Though unsuccessful in meeting the government's criteria, the United Houma Nation of south Louisiana, the Caddo-Adai of Robeline, the Clifton Choctaw west of Alexandria, and the Choctaw-Apache of Ebarb have been working the longest to gain recognition. Other groups of native people have begun seeking recognition more recently, such as the Biloxi-Chitimacha Muskogean Confederation.

Each federally recognized tribe has a unique relationship with the U.S. government and with the state government. In effect, they are on equal footing with a state and are answerable directly to Congress, not the state governor. Chitimacha chairman Alton D. LeBlanc, Jr., explains that sovereignty is affirmed in the U.S. Constitution: "Article 2, Section 8, clearly empowers the

U.S. Congress to have the power to regulate commerce of the states and the several Indian nations that reside within the borders of these states. The wisdom there, of the framers of the Constitution, was that there could be a real conflict to the detriment of tribes when a state would have authority or jurisdiction over an Indian tribe who historically had free and open rein in and out of this country."

This book attempts to shed light on the lives of the members of the sovereign nations in Louisiana. These are people who have lived through persecution, displacement, and forced assimilation, yet they retain their dignity. Though they maintain their cultural traditions in varying degrees, they are all proud of their heritage and seek to preserve and revive it. As Coushatta member Rayne Langley told us, "Everybody knows what the Cajun culture is. Now it's time for us to show ours." Their shared heritage makes them who they are, but they are not merely people of the past. They are people who are, and will be.

To learn about their present and future, we photographed and interviewed members of the four federally recognized tribes of Louisiana. We were drawn to them because these small tribes

are the only ones who have been able to meet the rigorous criteria for recognition. We were drawn to them because by that recognition, they are treated as their own nations. We were drawn to them because we are in awe.

We were met with sincerity and generosity. We found an overwhelming sense of honor among people who are convinced that regardless of their historical difficulties, they must face the future responsibly.

They have shared with us vivid elements of their histories. We hope people will hear through their voices these tribes' resolute strength of will and their outlooks for the future. This work cannot begin to tell all there is to know, but perhaps it can lead us closer to respect and under-standing.

The Chitimacha Tribe of Louisiana

To still walk this same land our ancestors walked. To again be able to care and provide for our people and those around us. To rekindle the pride in being Chitimacha. That is the greatest gift we can give our children.
—RALPH DARDEN, Chairman of the Chitimacha Tribe, 1989–1998

SK THE CHITIMACHA how long they have lived in Louisiana and the answer is simple: We have always been here. They trace their origin to a time when water covered the earth. The Great Spirit first created fish and shellfish, then commanded the crawfish to dive under the water and bring forth mud to fashion land. Next, He made man. He called the land and the men Chitimacha.

The Chitimacha thrived along the natural levees of the rivers and lakes of the vast Atchafalaya Basin for more than six thousand years. Though now reduced to less than three hundred acres, the Chitimacha are the only tribe in Louisiana that managed to retain even a portion of their ancestral lands. Tribal chairman Alton D. LeBlanc, Jr., says the land they occupy now was the highest ground in the area and logically the Chitimacha's main village site.

"Having held that ground—it wasn't an easy thing to do," explains LeBlanc, the depth of his conviction more evident with each word. "I like to look at that awesome thing as the fuel that fires the engine here. Just knowing what had to happen over the centuries to keep this where it is, and to keep us who we are—we don't have the right to give that up. It's not an option right now, not without dishonoring our ancestors. They certainly fully intended that we maintain our identity. I'm in awe that we are here."

Living peacefully for millennia, the Chitimacha flourished in what is now south Louisiana. They survived as fishermen, hunters, farmers, and basket makers and traded with the nearby Atakapa, Acolapissa, and Natchez tribes. The Chitimacha tribe grew to comprise at least twenty-nine villages and a population of more than twenty thousand people inhabiting most of the lower Mississippi River delta. By the early 1700s, the Chitimacha were the most powerful tribe of the northern Gulf Coast west of Florida.

Though the early Spanish explorers did little to change the tribe's way of life, the French were another matter. Assisted by Acolapissa and other tribes, French explorers raided the Chitimacha villages in the early 1700s and enslaved many women and children. When Chitimacha warriors set out in retaliation against these marauders, they encountered a small French trading party. Father Jean François Buisson de St. Cosme, the Jesuit missionary in the encampment, was killed along with the traders. His death incensed the French, who launched a devastating twelve-year war against the Chitimacha. The tribe sustained heavy losses in the fighting, which left only two major settlements west of the Mississippi River.

By the late 1700s, Acadians began flowing into the area. During this time European disease and assimilation slowly took their toll, diminishing the size of both the tribe and its land base.

From their first encounters, the French and Spanish governments dealt with the Chitimacha as a sovereign nation. With the Louisiana Purchase in 1803, the United States government affirmed that sovereignty—but largely in name only. Another century would pass before the United States government would formally recognize the Chitimacha and establish the present-day reservation. In the interim, tax disputes forced the sale of some of the tribe's land. By 1903, a court divided the remaining 461.68 acres, with the tribe retaining 261.54 acres. Basket making and farming were not enough to satisfy the attorney's fees, however, and Sarah Avery McIlhenny purchased the property at a sheriff's sale on the courthouse steps. She later asked the federal government to put the land into trust for the tribe. In 1916 President Woodrow Wilson signed the act that began the federal recognition process for the Chitimacha tribe. When the land was transferred to trust in 1919 and McIlhenny was reimbursed for the property, the recognition process was complete and the Chitimacha became the first federally recognized tribe in Louisiana.

Even as it received federal recognition, the tribe dwindled to a handful of families living along Bayou Teche and on Grand Lake. There they clung tenaciously to their old ways. But like the perennial spring floods, the mainstream culture continued to seep into their indigenous way of life.

Among the lost traditions were those practiced by medicine women Clara Darden and her adopted daughter, Delphine Stouff. Respected for her use of herbs and medicinal plants, Stouff's expertise in curing deadly snakebites was well known among the local medical community. When physicians wanted to learn her methods, Stouff willingly agreed. But when they balked at the prayers, she halted the instruction, for she knew that without the prayers the medicine would not work.

Stouff was also willing to work with a linguist to preserve the Chitimacha language. By 1932 Cajun French had nearly replaced the language, and only Stouff and former chief Benjamin Paul spoke Chitimacha fluently. Realizing that languages such as these were vanishing, Yale University linguist Morris Swadesh worked with the two elders to preserve the language on wax cylinders. Together they created an unprecedented two hundred hours of recordings.

Nearly sixty years later, the tribe began the monumental task of reawakening a language that no tribal member could speak. Finding a linguist who knew the isolate language was a challenge. Fortunately, they located Dr. Julian Granberry, who had explored connections between Chitimacha and the language of the Ais tribe of Florida. Granberry had taught himself Chitimacha as a young man, voraciously reading through Swadesh's materials. In 1997 he met with the tribe's elders to talk about the language. To test whether his knowledge and pronunciation of the language were correct, the tribe asked Granberry to speak in Chitimacha to the group. "He spoke to a group of elders, and tears came to their eyes," recalls Chitimacha cultural director Kimberly S. Walden. "We knew then that we had the right pronunciation."

From Swadesh's muddled, scratching wax cylinder recordings, Granberry devised learning materials for children and adults. The tribe stepped up its fight to resurrect the language, distributing the materials to every Chitimacha household from Louisiana to Germany. They instituted language classes to bring the ancient words to babies, grade school children, adults, and elders.

"The kids love it," Walden notes. "It's a great source of self-esteem for them, and it gives them pride in being Chitimacha." The people of the closely knit community near Charenton embrace learning their language with varying degrees of enthusiasm, but reviving their language makes them feel closer to their ancestors.

"It's really interesting to learn," says eighth-grade language student Arielle Darden. "My ancestors knew this. It's cool to learn what they knew."

The Chitimacha are adamant in their determination to nurture their language back into widespread use among the tribe. Reviving the language "helps you learn more about your tribal identity," Walden explains. "It's part of who you are."

Granberry agrees. "The only way you maintain a cultural viewpoint is through its language, because that's the way it talks. It only talks in terms that are meaningful to itself. You can't use English and still think in Chitimacha," the linguist insists. "In Chitimacha, you distinguish between the future and everything that came before. It's almost more of, 'We are focused on the future rather than present and past.'"

"What's happening here on this reservation is particularly unique. I have a feeling it will work here," Granberry says. "If it does, it will be the first time in the history of any Native American people in which a totally extinct language has been brought back to everyday use."

The Chitimacha's broad effort to reawaken their language comes at a time when languages the world over are declining. Of the 175 indigenous languages on this continent still spoken by at least a few members of the older generation 86 percent are not being learned by children.

"It's not our fault the language was lost," Walden clarifies. "When people are being shot in their front yards or being drug behind horses and hung, you lose what you have to, to survive."

Teachers Carolyn Burgess Savage and Sandra "Sam" Caro are on the front lines of today's language struggle. Through their efforts, tribal members see Chitimacha words on signs throughout the tribe's facilities, from the back of a preschooler's chair *(xux najipam)* in the

9

Yaamahana/Early Learning Center to a no smoking *(xicta gan)* sign in the recreational center. They signal that what started as a murmur is growing in resonance. The word lists based upon the recordings are growing as well, as elders continue to bring forth words shelved in the recesses of their memories.

Chairman LeBlanc says the language classes are part of the tribe's focus on its children, who embody the future of the Chitimacha. "It's our obligation to give our people a running start. We're doing everything we can, not only to preserve but revive parts of our culture that have been lost, because they're going to need every bit of it. The challenges to come will be exponentially greater," he explains.

The Chitimacha demonstrate their commitment to their children's future on a daily basis at the Chitimacha Tribal School, the only Indian primary school in the state. Walden says the school has always been significant to the tribe. "We fought to keep our school, even when we had low enrollment. It was important in the beginning, because we couldn't go to public school," she says. "Now, the tribe has control of their children's education. Our school system is very well funded, and the instruction is quite individualized, with five children in the smallest class."

Portraits of tribal leaders past and present line the school halls. The library boasts a special Native American section, while a few steps away tribal children explore the Internet in the school's computer lab. Tribal education has come a long way from earlier in the century. "They wouldn't let us Indians go to school, so the nuns at the convent taught us in a room separated from the regular kids," recalls Lester Darden, the eldest member of the tribe. An avid reader today, he quit school after second grade to work in the sugarcane and cornfields to help support his family.

Realizing education was critical to their survival, Chief Benjamin Paul sent twenty-one tribal members to the Carlisle Indian School in Pennsylvania in 1906. Ranging in age from ten to twenty-four years, the students enrolled for a mandatory five-year term. Once there, however, the schools separated the children from members of their tribe, forced them to speak English, threw their clothing away and gave them uniforms to wear. Native Americans who traditionally never cut their hair except in times of mourning had their hair lopped off.

"The conditions were deplorable. The students did more working than learning," says Walden. Caro agrees, noting that "a lot of them lost their spirit at those schools." Some students did, however, return to their tribe with the ability to read and write, as well as a trade skill. Educational opportunities were minimal in those years. Former chairman Leroy M. Burgess recalls starting school when he was twelve years old, when Chief Ernest "Papa Jack" Darden converted a room in his house into a classroom in 1932.

The Chitimacha were therefore thrilled to get their first school on the reservation in 1934—a one-room condemned black school building. Elder Nick Stouff remembers the occasion. "All the people got together and repaired it," Stouff says. "Then they got a teacher, and that thing stayed there for forty-odd years before they built the school they got here." The early school taught reading, writing, arithmetic, and basket making. The students and their parents planted a garden for food. Tribal members worked ceaselessly to keep the school in physical condition, but it was quickly overwhelmed with children.

"We had fifty-three kids in one room. Some were in the boiler room. If the heater went up, some of the kids could have been killed," recalls Burgess. Tribal leaders explained the situation to officials in Washington, who in the end provided nearly a million dollars to fund the building of a new and larger school. In 1978 the new school finally opened on tribal lands, providing kindergarten to eighth-grade classes for eighty students by 1999.

School Principal Tanya Rosamond is proud of the quality instruction the school's students receive. Framed by moss-covered oaks, the modern brick school follows state and federal curriculum guidelines while still offering lessons specific to the Chitimacha culture. The students' performance on standardized tests is above that of St. Mary Parish and the state of Louisiana. After tribal members attend the high school of their choice, those who wish to attend college receive enthusiastic support from the tribe, which will provide funds for tuition, books, and some living expenses. In return for scholarships, students work in tribal offices and community activities, performing "payback hours."

Today's Chitimacha have a myriad of choices when it comes to careers. In years past, tribal members on the ancestral lands worked along the bayous and lakes fishing and gathering moss sold to make mattresses. "Life was hard out on the lake, but there was always fish to eat," recalls Lester Darden. "We used a trotline, caught catfish and gaspagoo that we fried or made into sauce piquante."

With few educational opportunities—no Chitimacha from the reservation graduated from public high school until 1962—and little employment available to them locally, many tribal members left the area in search of better jobs. Often they found employment in the Louisiana oil fields, eventually becoming drillers, foremen, and even rig captains.

Many tribal members chose to enlist in the military, eager to protect the land that had always been theirs. In 1942, Leroy Burgess and his brother, Norwood, joined the Marines just before their eighth-grade graduation. Leroy earned two Purple Hearts and a Silver Star in World War II. Nearly seventy tribal members became veterans, including nine who served in World War I and twenty who served in World War II.

After returning from the war, Leroy Burgess found himself appointed to a temporary council in 1948. The tribe had come close to establishing a constitutional form of government in 1932 and again in 1946. Their third attempt in 1948 ran headlong into the federal government's policy of termination of federal services to Indians. By 1969, the tribe's intentions were not to be denied. "We had to have a document by which we could conduct business with the federal government and state government. We had guidelines from the Bureau of Indian Affairs. A lot was copied, and a lot was our work. We had high school to grade school people trying to put up a constitution. We got it on paper, had it ratified by the membership, had it approved by the commissioner and that put us in business. It's the same constitution that we live by today to transact business," Burgess explains.

After sending it to numerous government officials for approval, Burgess says the tribe quickly tired of having to make minor changes to appease nontribal bureaucrats. "By that time I was kind of getting upset over it," recalls Burgess. "When it got back the second time, I said, 'Who are we preparing this thing for?' Well, I said, 'If we're preparing it for us, let's just sign it and send it off and see what happens.'"

Constitution writers Burgess, Nick Stouff, Leslie Proctor, Alvin Vilcan, and Archie Vilcan did just that. The tribe took a major step in self-determination with the constitution's approval, electing a council under its provisions by 1971.

Burgess became chairman shortly after and set about finding ways to propel the tribe into a more secure future. At eighty, Burgess quietly exhibits the no-nonsense, candid outlook that helped his tribe move forward. "I got the Federal Register and found out about programs we could vie for, that had never been mentioned to us," Burgess remembers. The tribe's initiative in working with agencies such as the Bureau of Indian Affairs allowed housing issues to be addressed first, followed quickly by health care. By the mid-1980s the tribe was recreating itself, becoming a role model in providing community services.

Chairman LeBlanc notes that the tribe's success in making improvements for its members is rooted in its ability to arm itself with information. "An MO for us is to know the book better than the BIA [Bureau of Indian Affairs]," he says with a smile. "That's how we've made great strides. Whether it's an inquiry, a grant application—we do it from a base of knowledge, and it's pretty intimidating to bureaucrats."

By 1993, the tribe took advantage of changes in federal law to convert bingo operations to a casino, which substantially improved the tribe's financial situation. The vibrant colors of Cypress Bayou Casino burst from the surrounding sugarcane fields. The casino boasts among its amenities Mr. Lester's, a world-class steakhouse named for Lester Darden. Its impact on local employment is immense, as the venture pays out $25 million in payroll in the area each year and employs approximately 1,030 people, only about 25 of whom are tribal members. After regulatory and other expenses are covered, 50 percent of the revenues are used to run Chitimacha tribal government. The tribe distributes the remaining 50 percent directly to its more than one thousand members.

Much as the Chitimacha once taught incoming settlers to live off the land, today's Chitimacha nourish the local economy with the casino. Under a community grant agreement, the tribe gives the parish, St. Mary Parish Sheriff's Office, and five municipalities $1.5 million a year. "The outer communities are able to capitalize on the renaissance of this tribe," LeBlanc notes.

As a result, both tribal and local parish governments have much to celebrate. Casino revenues combine with federal grants and other tribal enterprises to fund the enhancement of a wealth of services for tribal members. A state-of-the-art medical center, including a pharmacy, laboratory, and dental and radiology services, opened in 1999 with a physician on the premises.

The tribe is proud of its tribal court building, assisted living center for the tribe's elders, and Yaamahana/Early Learning Center. Inside the learning center, elders walk over a blackbird's-eye basket design incorporated into the floor. They are on their way to rock the babies and hope to sing songs to them in Chitimacha. The Yaamahana unites the old with the new in many ways. The spacious building features modern architectural highlights, while legends of the sun and the moon, the sacred rain tree, and the eagle circle the outer wall on concrete tiles made by the tribe's children.

Reminders of the tribe's heritage also fill the tribe's newly renovated museum. Upon entering, visitors encounter a mannequin of Chief Framboise, who led the tribe at the end of the Chitimacha-French war. A push of a button prompts him to welcome guests to the main village site in the Chitimacha language.

The centerpieces of the museum's exhibits are the strikingly intricate river cane baskets for which the Chitimacha are acclaimed. The basket making tradition continues today because in 1899 Clara Darden created a very large collection of baskets, with many traditional Chitimacha designs. She taught the art to the young Chitimacha women and girls in hopes of keeping the tradition alive. Only four people carry on basketry in the twenty-first century, however, as jobs outside the home take precedence. Melissa Darden takes the time to weave baskets the way her grandmother, Lydia Darden, taught her, but she also attends college and is a supervisor at the tribe's casino. Melissa's brother, John Paul Darden, also weaves the baskets, as does his wife, Scarlette.

John Paul Darden brings his tribal knowledge and thirteen years of basket making experience to his position as the curator for the Chitimacha Museum. He can share stories about artisans past and present while explaining their differing techniques. He points out many of the numerous and complex yet whimsical designs unique to Chitimacha baskets, including the perch design, eye of cattle, bird's eye in a square block, and alligator entrails. He takes a moment to say each design name in the Chitimacha language as well, spoken with "impeccable pronunciation," Granberry cheerily proclaims. Darden says the painstakingly crafted Chitimacha baskets, including the double-weave methods of Raymond Thomas, are in great demand from private collectors and museums around the world. "People from everywhere want our baskets solely because they are Chitimacha baskets. If we sat down to weave for the next two years, we wouldn't catch up," he explains.

Though the tribe's basket makers can command healthy prices for their work, their baskets do not support them. Neither do their per-capita distributions from the casino revenue. "By and large, people use their annual per-capita distribution for home improvements and other amenities to improve their quality of life," LeBlanc says.

The casino has fueled the tribe's economic upswing, but tribal members continue to look to the future. Chairman LeBlanc is quick to point out that economic diversification plans include a master-plan community. In researching development opportunities, he explains, the Chitimacha found that housing was a critical need for the area. With their experience in building their own community, the Chitimacha found a perfect fit. The master-plan community is dubbed Raintree Village, in honor of the legend of the sacred cypress rain tree. During periods of severe drought, a sprig from the holy tree was dipped into the water. Legend says that this would always bring rain.

The master-plan community will be located along Ralph Darden Memorial Parkway, named after the previous chairman whose efforts brought the tribe to its current economic prosperity. The residential development will include supporting commercial sites such as a grocery store, bank, gas station and other retail businesses. The tribe allowed the town of Baldwin to incorporate the land, doubling the size of the town and its tax base.

LeBlanc notes that though the tribe made a conscious decision "not to build walls around this 260 acres," his main objective is still for the tribe to retain its distinct identity. "The native history that is here will continue to be here as long as it's in the hearts of the people," he explains. "We need to teach our children to be comfortable with themselves, with their Chitimacha heritage, and their French heritage if it's French, or English or Irish or whatever that may be. No matter what the blood quantum is, that heritage will live on," he vows. "We are a unique tribe that's always been here. We've lost so many people over the centuries, whether it was through wars with the French or other tribes or disease. A lot of things happened through the centuries that caused us to be the small group that we are. But we are at the main village site, the one that's been here forever."

As tribal elder Lester Darden succinctly puts it, "I was born a Chitimacha. I'll die a Chitimacha."

Clara Darden is responsible for the turn-of-the-century revival of Chitimacha basketry. With the help of Mary M. Bradford of Avery Island, she produced a collection of 72 baskets that showcases many of the Chitimacha basket designs. Clara's father, Jean Alexandre Dardenne, Jr., was the last lineage chief. As tribal tradition allowed daughters and sons of chiefs to marry only someone of their own status, Clara remained single. Born in 1800, Clara died at the age of 110. (Courtesy Peabody Museum, Harvard University.)

For centuries the Chitimacha thrived in the lakes and bayous of the Atchafalaya Basin. According to tribal legend, Chitimacha warriors fought courageously in an epic battle to rid the land of a huge and venomous snake. The beast turned and twisted for days in a slow death, deepening the place where its body lay, creating the bayou named Teche, Chitimacha for snake. The curve of Bayou Teche known today as Indian Bend flows past the Chitimacha reservation.

Wearing a traditional Chitimacha shirt, tribal chairman Alton D. LeBlanc, Jr., sits among cypress trees on Lake Fausse Point.

"THERE'S QUITE A COMMITMENT in the community to preserve our heritage. We as tribal members don't have a choice in the matter. Our ancestors fought long and hard to remain this identifiable group of people. It would be a slap in their faces to give up on that, especially now that we have the resources to revive and preserve our culture."

When the Chitimacha's last medicine woman, Delphine Stouff, passed away in 1940, many of the Chitimacha's healing ways were lost. But her voice lives on in wax cylinder recordings of the Chitimacha language made from 1932 to 1934. Stouff was one of the last two fluent speakers of the Chitimacha language. (Courtesy National Museum of the American Indian, Smithsonian Institution, P12200. Photograph by Mark R. Harrington.)

The home of Chief Ben Paul, shown here in the early 1900s, saw much of the tribe's recent history. Chief Paul and his wife, Christine, opened their home to the orphans of the tribe. In 1905, expectant mother Virginia Paul Darden was one of three Chitimacha murdered in the front yard of the home. Virginia's husband, Jules Darden, was murdered in 1908. Chief Paul and his wife raised the Dardens' orphaned son, Arthur, and Arthur's son Ralph became a much beloved tribal chairman in 1989. (Courtesy National Anthropological Archives, Smithsonian Institution, 74-901.)

Chitimacha tribal elder Lester Darden takes in the view of Bayou Teche from his bedroom window. To tribal members "Uncle Lester," born in 1908, was a well-respected source of the history of the tribe until his death in 2002.

Though their parents were once forbidden to learn their language, Chitimacha tribal elders Janet Martin (left) and Heloise Lange (right) now learn words that bring back memories of their ancestors during a language class taught by cultural community instructor Carolyn Burgess Savage.

"IT'S HARD TO TEACH our language while you are still learning. You're just a step ahead. It never occurred to us that we couldn't teach and learn at the same time, but that is exactly what we are doing. It is a struggle. Most people drop out before they get to where these elders are. I admire them so much for their commitment."

Chitimacha Tribal School second-grade students (from left) Philbert Schexnaider, Jessie Dautreuil, and Kevin Hebert learn the Chitimacha language as cultural instructor Sandra "Sam" Caro uses Beanie Babies to demonstrate Chitimacha words.

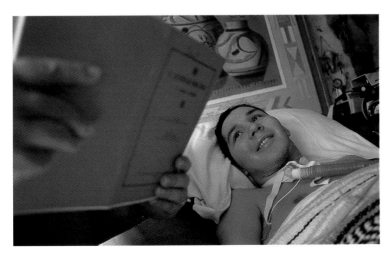

Though paralyzed from a motorcycle accident, Bret Burgess still aspires to learn the Chitimacha language. The tribe offers language classes to all members at the tribal school, the Early Learning Center, and the Cultural Department.

Chitimacha tribal member Craig Burgess chips the center from a cottonwood log as he helps build a traditional Chitimacha dugout. The primary means of transport in the Atchafalaya Basin, dugouts were made from either cottonwood or cypress and could hold as many as 30 people.

The Chitimacha Tribal School welcomes students from other area schools during its 4-H Club Cultural Exchange Day. Visitors witness Native American traditions like tribal school student Erin Compton twirling to the beat of the drum. The "drum" for the fancy shawl dance is THUNDERHORSE, made up of members of the Coushatta and other tribes.

Students stomp moss into mud during a Cultural Exchange Day demonstration of traditional palmetto hut construction.

Nervousness battles with excitement in the lobby of the Chitimacha Tribal School as kindergarten students Elizabeth Butaud and Dallas Brown wait for the opening procession of commencement ceremonies for graduating kindergarten and eighth-grade students.

Chitimacha Tribal School students continue their education at local public or private schools or at Native American schools such as Sequoyah High School in Tahlequah, Oklahoma. Tribal members (from left) Zachary LeBlanc, April Cook, Jared Anslum, and Ashley Burgess stand in the lobby of Hanson Memorial High School, a local Catholic school.

Chitimacha tribal scholarships allow (from left) Dina S. Lucas, Nikina V. Burgess, Bruce Burgess, and Narissa Miguez to attend the University of Louisiana at Lafayette. Coming full circle, tribal members pay the tribe back through community service. But Ms. Burgess believes payback should not end there.

"**THEY SHOULD ALWAYS** try to come back here and better the tribe after they get a good education. It's important to come back here to share the knowledge that you gained, to share it with our community to help keep our community strong."

In the early 1900s many Chitimacha families lived on Grand Lake. Today, Chitimacha tribal members like Vernon "Bubba" Higgins and Henry "Skippy" Sedatol, Jr., continue to fish in the lakes and bayous. Here they shovel their catch of shad at Chitimacha Seafood and Bait Co.

Russell Persilver, Jr., weighs a sack of crawfish brought in by local fishermen. Persilver buys crawfish and catfish at the Chitimacha Seafood and Bait Co. processing plant. "I've been at this so long, I don't really want to stop," he says. "I try to keep it going. Some years are good and some years are no good at all." Persilver laments that though his entire family has been fishing all of their lives, his kids won't have anything to do with it.

Chitimacha tribal member John Burgess patrols the reservation for the Chitimacha Police Department. Burgess admits that though the close-knit ties of the reservation make him welcome in all homes, it can make enforcement difficult.

"I CHOSE MY CAREER, my lifestyle, in honor of my father, Harvey Burgess, Sr. Regardless of how bad I was when I was younger, he always told me, if you put your heart forward there is nothing you cannot achieve. I want to pass that legacy to my child, teach him the ways of my father. I must do what is right each and every time."

Tribal member Pam Darden Thibodeaux works at a controlled burn in a sugarcane field. Part of her role with the Chitimacha Fire Protection is teaching fire prevention to tribal youth, and she hopes they learn from her that opportunities never end. She is evidence of that herself, earning her GED with her daughter in 1995, nearly 20 years after quitting high school. She took to heart the wishes of her late uncle, tribal chairman Ralph Darden.

"[CHAIRMAN DARDEN] ALWAYS pushed tribal members to continue to grow, to make yourself more than what you are. . . . If it weren't for the tribe stressing the importance of education, I don't think I would have gone [back to school]. If I hadn't moved here to the reservation, I wouldn't be where I am today. Living here pushed me to go further."

Tribal member Marty Burgess.

U.S. Navy veteran Craig Burgess bows his head during Veterans Day ceremonies at the Chitimacha Tribal School. Many tribal members are veterans, including 6 who served in World War I and 24 who served in World War II.

Chitimacha tribal elder Leroy M. Burgess served his country in World War II, earning two Purple Hearts and the Silver Star in his 29 months of service in the Pacific theater while assigned to the 2nd Marine Division. In a 76-hour battle to capture the airfield at Tarawa in the Gilbert Islands, Burgess earned his Silver Star for resourcefulness in penetrating a crucial machine gunner's nest.

General Douglas MacArthur, center, meets with Native American men on Goodenough Island in 1943, including Chitimacha tribal member Staff Sgt. Alvin J. Vilcan (left) and Navajo Sgt. Byron L. Tsinajine. The men were part of the 158th Regimental Combat Team, which included Indians from 20 different tribes. Vilcan, later a tribal constitution writer, overcame a lack of education in his youth to start his own business. (Courtesy U.S. Army Signal Corps.)

In 1970 the Chitimacha tribe completed its 35-year effort to draft a tribal constitution and bylaws. Tribal elders (from left) Nick Stouff, Archie Vilcan, Leslie Proctor, and Leroy M. Burgess proudly hold a copy of the Chitimacha constitution that they and Alvin Vilcan (not shown) wrote.

"AT THE TIME that we wrote the constitution, that's when sovereign nations were being declared all over the United States. . . . We had to have a constitution that declared our sovereignty. It means that you can't be bullied by just anybody around you. You have protection. That's what happened to the Chitimacha nation to begin with: we didn't have the constitution and sovereignty, and we lost the majority of our land in Louisiana."

—Archie Vilcan

Peeking from under the election booth curtains, Katie Martin joins her father, Gerry Martin, during tribal elections. The tribe has participated vigorously in elections ever since the tribal constitution and bylaws were approved in 1971.

Rising out of the surrounding sugarcane fields in St. Mary Parish, Cypress Bayou Casino has improved the finances of the Chitimacha Nation. Casino revenue has enhanced a wealth of social and civic services, including cultural preservation efforts.

Concrete tiles handmade by Chitimacha Tribal School students adorn the Yaamahana, the Chitimacha's early learning center. Each child was asked to create a design that represented Chitimacha to them, and the results included renderings of legends, oral histories, tribal activities, and traditional tribal homes.

With growing prosperity the Chitimacha Nation continues to expand facilities and services for its members. In November 1999 tribal council members (from left) Toby Darden, Peggy Darden Gaddy, Chairman Alton D. LeBlanc, Jr., and Lonnie Martin proudly cut the ribbon to open the tribe's new medical center.

Chitimacha tribal elders, from left, Helen Mora, Cora Vilcan, Seniolla Proctor, and Dot Newman watch the Thanksgiving feast ribbon-cutting ceremony of the tribe's new medical facility.

Secrets are irresistible to children around the world, and it's no different at a swim meet at the Chitimacha Aquatic Facility. Chitimacha swimmer Hannah LaGarde listens as Lindsey Martin whispers into her ear before a relay event during a swim meet. The Chitimacha swim team is one of many popular Chitimacha recreational programs, including golf, soccer, track, volleyball, softball, and basketball.

Evening horseplay begins as Chitimacha track team members (from left) Jolby Schexnaider, Brandt Johnson, Matthew Darden, Nicholas Persilver, Tasia Bernard, Morgan Martin, and Grant Lagarde gather after a meet at Franklin Senior High School.

Tribal member Terry Martin drives a ball from a bunker on Le Triomphe golf course during the Nike Louisiana Open. The tribe sponsors the event to raise money for local charities and "increase the sense of community," Chairman LeBlanc explains. "We want to encourage other groups, organizations, and even communities to join in and help those in need."

Tribal members (from left) Scarlette Darden, Melissa Darden, and John Paul Darden display their baskets in front of the home of former chief Ben Paul. Melissa says she pestered her grandmother to teach her the difficult craft until finally her grandmother said, "Here, you take this cane and peel it, and if you can peel it, then I will show you." Today Melissa is one of four basket makers in the tribe.

This double-weave basket shows a snake design with straight worm tracks on the lid. The river cane *(piya)* is gathered locally, split, peeled, then dried and dyed in the traditional Chitimacha colors of yellow *(qijitem)*, red *(pinun)*, and black *(napxjin)*.

Battling heat and summer boredom, tribal member Clay Burgess plays on a trampoline at the home of Heloise Mora.

Like the nearby communities of Jeanerette, Coteau, and Lore-auville, the Chitimacha hold their own Mardi Gras parade, which winds through the reservation. Tribal member Needron Bernard blasts foam toward the judges' stand as his "lunar module" float drives by. The parade started with the Chitimacha Tribal School children on the school grounds and grew into a full-blown community parade.

Porch gathering sustains the sense of community as the families of Roy Darden and his sister Elaine Dwyer gather at Darden's home on the Chitimacha reservation. "We live life as one big family out here because we *are* one big family," says Chairman LeBlanc.

The Tunica-Biloxi Tribe of Louisiana

We're a proud people. We're an honorable people. We take pride in our cultural heritage and take a special interest in working with our local community to make this parish a better place to live for all our kids. Although the past is very important to us, our future is also very important.

— EARL BARBRY, SR., Chairman of the Tunica-Biloxi Tribe

AS ONE TRAVELS ALONG Louisiana Highway 1 southeast of Marksville, swampy floodplains give way to cotton fields that stretch as far as the eye can see. For years, the Tunica-Biloxi Indian reservation was barely noticeable among these fields. Only a few tribal families remained, finding what work they could in the surrounding fields and bayous.

But this tribe has always found a way to adapt to ensure its survival. Three hundred years ago, that meant leading the salt and horse trades in the lower Mississippi delta. In Marksville, it has meant breaking down barriers between the tribe and local governments. It has meant improving the standard of living for all tribal members. Today it means that the fields along Highway 1 are the backdrop for a bustling economy driven by the tribe's casino resort.

Leading the tribe through these changes is Earl Barbry, Sr., who comes from a line of Indian chiefs but never intended to go into politics himself. Barbry was busy working and raising his family when he learned the tribe had crafted a deal with the city of Marksville to rent the reservation as a garbage dump. In exchange, the tribe would receive fifty dollars a month and a road would be built onto the reservation. When Barbry attended a tribal meeting where the deal was to be approved, he didn't think it was a good deal. "I guess because so many of our people were raised in poverty, fifty dollars seemed like a lot. This was discussed, how it would be good for the tribe," he recalls. Then it was his turn to speak. "I just reminded them how the city had treated them all their lives, like trash, and now they wanted to allow them to dump their trash on our land," he says. Barbry says his love of the land is more than just property ownership: "This is the only thing that keeps us apart from everybody else. This is our nation."

By the end of the meeting, the decision to reject the dump proposal was made, and Barbry's entry into politics seemed a foregone conclusion. Shortly after, he was appointed to fill an unexpired tribal council term as vice chairman. In 1978, he became chairman and has been reelected to that post ever since.

One of his main goals as chairman has been to strengthen the relationships between the tribe and the city, parish, and state. As a sovereign nation, the tribe governs itself and answers directly to the federal government. "When I first took office, I wanted to establish a good working relationship with the people here, and I think it has paid off," Barbry explains. "Although we're a sovereign entity, that's not something that I've ever tried to force down [other local governments'] throats. I let them know about it. The injustices that have been done to the people here is not something I dwell on, and I encourage my people not to do it. Rather we're all part of the same community, and I want to work together to make a good place for our kids to grow up."

The tribe's recognition as a sovereign nation was slow in coming. The process began with Chief Eli Barbry, Earl's paternal grandfather, who made his way to Washington, D.C., with a handful of tribal members in a Model T Ford. The efforts that began with the tribe's leaders in the 1930s finally yielded formal recognition from the federal government in 1981.

"It's really sad, all of these older people like my parents, Chief Joe [Pierite], and some of the older ones. I can remember when we had get-togethers, that's what the discussion was—how much better things would be once we got federally recognized. They all looked forward to that, but by the time it happened, quite a few of them had passed on. They were all deceased by the time of the casino. They weren't able to see the benefits of all they had worked for. But they never gave up," Barbry recalls. "I wish a lot of our elders could be here to enjoy the fruits of their hard work. I can remember when I was real young how much it meant, all the hope they had."

Today's Tunica-Biloxi Indians of Louisiana owe a lot to those who have gone before. Although it's not obvious from his small, unassuming office with piles of paperwork covering his desk, Barbry now leads a tribe involved in multimillion-dollar business ventures. Each tribal member is a part owner of those ventures, and their ownership is due in no small part to their elders' efforts to gain federal recognition of the tribe and to the handful of families who stayed on the reservation when others left to seek work elsewhere during the Depression years. Because those seven or eight families stayed, the tribe remained intact, which helped them gain their long-sought recognition.

These Indians, who were raised poor and "didn't know there was anything better," Barbry says, have come through their adversity successfully. The Tunica-Biloxi's business entities in Marksville now stand like sparkling jewels in the fields of central Louisiana. The Las Vegas–style Paragon Casino Resort, which includes a hotel and the Tamahka Trails golf course, is joined by an RV park, and further amenities are planned to continue bringing economic viability to the area.

From their first documented contact with Europeans in the sixteenth century, the Tunica Indians have historically met challenges by moving forward. In 1541, Spanish explorer Hernando de Soto encountered them in Quizquiz, a noted center of power in northwestern Mississippi above the confluence of the Mississippi and Arkansas rivers. The Spaniards were accustomed to bloody conflicts with Indians, but upon confronting nearly four thousand armed warriors they decided peacemaking might be a better option at Quizquiz.

Famine, warfare, and the onslaught of European diseases nearly decimated the tribe and prompted them to move from Quizquiz. The French encountered the Tunica on the Yazoo River at its junction with the Mississippi in 1699. The Tunica then steadily made themselves indispensable to the French as political and military allies and through their control of the vital salt trade.

Unrest in the Yazoo region, including a British-instigated Chickasaw raid, drove the Tunica from the area in 1706. They continued their southern trek, this time bypassing their old rivals, the Natchez, to settle in the vicinity of the Red River's confluence with the Mississippi. They once again controlled the salt trade from there until one of the greatest disasters in Tunica history occurred. The Natchez, who had been defeated by the French, chose to seek retribution from the Tunica for their political alignments. Under the pretense of making peace, the Natchez had the French arrange a meeting that both tribes would attend unarmed. Under cover of night, the Natchez instead slaughtered the Tunica's chief and many of the tribe. After the destruction the Tunica moved again, this time a few miles south to a site now known as Trudeau, Louisiana. Once again, the tribe not only adapted to its surroundings but found a way to take control of its destiny. At Trudeau, the tribe continued to control trade where the Red River met the Mississippi. Here they also strengthened their position in the crucial horse trade, as they were located even closer to French settlements.

In the 1770s, the Tunica moved to Marksville on the Red River. The tribe remains today on the land granted to them by Spanish authorities. Bureau of Indian Affairs records show that the current tribe is the result of a gradual fusion of the Tunica, Ofo, Avoyel, and Biloxi tribes in Marksville, which probably culminated in about 1810. Each of these tribes had continually documented interactions with the French and Spanish authorities throughout the 1700s. The United States government formally recognized the combined Tunica-Biloxi Tribe of Louisiana in 1981, attesting that they have maintained both their cultural identity and tribal governments throughout their history.

The Tunica's trading acumen throughout their history is evidenced through the collection of artifacts in the Tunica Treasure. The size of the collection as well as the quality of the items acquired through trade attests to the tribe's business savvy. The Tunica Treasure is especially clear evidence of the importance of the Tunica tribe to the French, who looked upon the tribe as a key ally for many, many years.

"The Tunica Treasure is one of the things that means more to me than the casino or anything else," Chairman Barbry says. "We were able to recover and preserve the artifacts that were taken from our ancestors' graves. That is very important." Though the tribe's members were aware their ancestors had occupied the area of Trudeau, Louisiana, near the modern-day site of Angola State Penitentiary, they had no idea that a guard from the prison had located their burial ground and had been ransacking the graves. They learned of it from the State of Louisiana, which asked that the tribe intervene in the case of *Charrier v. Bell* to try to keep the artifacts from being sold. Barbry readily agreed, on the condition that the artifacts be returned to the tribe.

"Leonard Charrier was trying to improve his lot in life," says Donald Juneau, one of the attorneys who handled the ensuing litigation for the tribe. Charrier had stocked his home with the artifacts before filing suit against the owner of the land to claim half of what he unearthed. Charrier's luck turned, though, when the courts ruled in 1983 that he never owned the collection of artifacts because the items were never given up for ownership. "It was buried with these people and was not intended to be dug up or sold," Juneau explains. "The judge brought the case to what it was, a case of abandonment. And these goods were never abandoned."

The tribe built an underground museum in anticipation of the artifacts' arrival, thus creating a symbolic burial site for the items once taken from their ancestors' graves. When the items arrived, they were severely deteriorated. "The artifacts were in bad shape, with bronze disease and rusting pots falling apart," recalls Barbry's son, Earl junior, who leads conservation efforts and directs the museum. "We wondered how we'd fill up the building, but once we got the items we didn't wonder anymore. There was an orange glow in the room, there was so much rust." The tribe created a conservation lab with its few resources, transforming refrigerated eighteen-wheeler trailers into controlled environments suitable for artifact storage and restoration processes.

"Because of what we were able to do and the stand we took in preserving those artifacts, there was federal legislation enacted—the Native American Graves Protection and Repatriation Act—that's in place now," Chairman Barbry explains. By establishing that grave goods belong to descendants, the Tunica case laid the groundwork for the federal law, which requires that grave goods and other items that can be identified as belonging to a particular tribe and are held by museums and federal and state agencies, must be returned to the tribe from which they came.

Barbry says that while his tribe takes care to cherish the past, it is also looking to the future. As conservators continue their work in the museum, across the street the tribe's leaders continue their quest to provide the best for the tribe. Since 1981, the chairman and tribal council have used the benefits of tribal recognition to upgrade facilities on the reservation and enhance the tribe's standard of living through housing and health-care assistance. Thirteen years after gaining recognition, the tribe opened the Grand Casino Avoyelles resort casino on tribal lands. Revenue from the casino has allowed the tribe to branch out into other business ventures, including fast-food franchises in the area. Successful business ventures have made it possible to broaden the tribe's 132-acre land base to a total holding of more than 1,300 acres and to pursue claims on thousands of additional acres.

A per-capita check every month for members has helped raise their individual standard of living, and in addition, the tribe now provides college tuition to any tribal member seeking to further his or her education. New revenues have also prompted creation of a broad range of social services for the tribe, as well as a housing authority. This prosperity has brought distant tribal members back to the reservation and surrounding communities. "What was considered improper and shunned—being a member of the tribe—is now coveted and frequently requested," says the younger Barbry, a council member as well as museum director.

Tunica-Biloxi Pow Wow organizer John Barbry is one of those tribal members who moved back to the reservation once the tribe's economy improved. "I thought to do a pow wow would be a good thing, to introduce my people to tribes that were continuing their traditions—to look within themselves and within their history to try to revive things that only the elders knew anything about," he says. "It became apparent that it was one of the few times during the year that our tribal members could come together in a social setting, more of a celebration."

Marshall Pierite, director of social services for the Tunica-Biloxi, notes that financial stability has allowed the tribe to search for opportunities to familiarize its members with their heritage. One such project is the tribe's four-week camp each summer for children ages six to eighteen. "They learn the ancient language, tribal history, and cultural traditions," Pierite says. "We're really trying to revive our culture. We're not actually living within our traditions."

Earl Barbry, Jr., notes that the tribe's economic success under his father's lengthy leadership pales only in comparison to the tribe's era as powerful traders, when the famed Tunica Treasure was amassed. But the tribe's chairman doesn't believe that's enough. "If the need is there, you need to do whatever it takes to meet that need," Barbry states firmly. "In this type of industry, it's continually changing. If you stop, you're finished. There's always someone who will try to outdo you. To keep what you have, you must keep making improvements."

Always looking to the future, the tribe has made plans to ensure its continuing prosperity. The tribe has recently completed a new expansion of its hotel, with more growth projected. Tribal leaders are discussing plans for an industrial park, a new lab and museum, and possibly a movie theater and bowling alley.

The Tunica-Biloxi's reach has extended far beyond the Avoyelles Parish line, however. The tribe is working in California and New Mexico and on the East Coast to help other tribes duplicate their successes. The tribe's casino development and management company, First Nations Gaming Corporation, recently completed its third casino project. First Nations has now developed casinos in Valley Center, California; Santa Clara, New Mexico; and San Diego County, California and is currently working with a tribe in Massachusetts. Meanwhile, the tribe, which now owns 51 percent of the company, is also negotiating with the other owners to acquire full ownership.

The psychological impact of the tribe's financial success is not to be ignored, Chairman Barbry says. Tribal members "can take pride in saying they are a member of the tribe, where before I think they weren't [as proud]," the tribe's leader says. In addition, "it's stirred up a little bit more interest in their culture." Barbry firmly believes that that pride is well placed because it is the tribe's members who have made the tribe's success possible. He recalled an attorney who once questioned him on the most valuable asset the tribe had, expecting to hear "the casino" as the answer. Barbry told him that the most valuable thing the tribe has is its people. "If we didn't have our people, we wouldn't have anything else," he explained.

"It takes not only the chairman or the council, it takes all of our people to make things happen," the chairman says. "If we don't have their support it doesn't happen. There have been a lot of changes in the tribal council, but we've always moved forward."

The daughter of Chief Horace Pierite and Marceline Chiqui Pierite, Carrie Pierite Barbry was born on May 13, 1906. She lived to see the tribe finally attain federal recognition in 1981, though she died months later. Carrie and her husband Sam Barbry had five sons and one daughter. As tribal chariman, their son Earl has led the Tunica-Biloxi tribe into the next century. (Courtesy Mr. and Mrs. Earl J. Barbry, Sr.)

Chairman Earl Barbry, Sr., embarks on another term of office. One of the longest serving leaders in tribal history, Barbry has been chairman since 1978.

"SOVEREIGNTY IS THE RIGHT to govern ourselves. We choose our own destiny. The only entity we answer to is the federal government. We govern just like any other nation. We always have been [a nation], but the only problem is not everyone recognized that. . . . We were recognized by the French, the Spanish, and the British; the United States government was the last one to recognize us and our rights."

A tribal member slips a vote into the ballot box as Lula Cryer (left) and Opal Blanco anticipate their turn. The tribe's sovereignty is taken seriously by Tunica-Biloxi tribal members. Nearly all eligible tribal members participate in the elections, including those who live in far-off locations such as Houston and Chicago.

A packed council meeting room erupts into applause as election results are announced. As Alfred Barbre (far left) learns he will be the tribe's vice chairman, tribal members Joe and Juanita Barbre Banse join in the applause.

Using casino revenue to invest in other businesses, the Tunica-Biloxi tribe operates several fast-food franchises, including this Burger King next to the casino and three other Burger Kings in Many, Winnfield, and Jonesboro.

Towering above Louisiana Highway 1, Paragon Casino Resort includes a Las Vegas–style casino, a golf course, an RV park, and a hotel. Paragon is the foundation of the Tunica-Biloxi tribe's economic development plans.

Roy Pierite directs a cement truck in construction of golf cart paths for the tribe's new Tamahka Trails Golf Club near Paragon Casino Resort. *Tamahka* is the Tunica word for alligator. "I'm very proud to be a member of the tribe," says Pierite, who has owned his own company, T&R Construction, since 1997. Pierite says he is living much better now that the tribe has experienced prosperity.

Predawn light quietly silhouettes the former Tunica-Biloxi Museum, an earthen mound that mirrors the form of ancient temples. The Tunica trace their heritage back to the prehistoric Mississippian culture and the fabled town of Quizquiz. In 1541 Hernando de Soto arrived at Quizquiz, above the confluence of the Arkansas and Mississippi rivers. He and his men began ravaging the town, but when faced with thousands of warriors they soon sought peace.

"OFF TO ONE SIDE of the town was the dwelling place of the *curaca* [chief]. It was situated on a high mound which now served as a fortress. Only by means of two stairways could one ascend to this house. Here many Indians gathered while others sought refuge in a very wild forest lying between the town and the Great River. The lord of the province, who like his land was called Quizquiz, was now old and sick in bed; but on hearing the noise and confusion in his village, he arose and came from his bedchamber. Then beholding the pillage and the seizure of his vassals, he grasped a battle-ax and began to descend the stairs with the greatest fury, in the meantime vowing loudly and fiercely to slay anyone who came into his land without permission."

—EL INCA GARCILASO DE LA VEGA, Peruvian-born Spanish soldier, translator, and historian

Alligators guard the entrance of the Tunica-Biloxi Museum, just as alligators guarded a hole in the earth in a story of the tribe's origin. Legend has it that when the Tunica recited a special prayer, the alligators moved aside, allowing the Tunica to move out into the world.

Dedicated to preserving the Tunica Treasure, tribal members and conservators Earl Barbry, Jr. (left), and his cousin Brent Barbry dip a copper kettle into a wax bath. The Tunica Treasure is an extraordinary collection of European and Native artifacts stolen from ancestral burial sites at Trudeau, just south of the Louisiana state penitentiary at Angola. Now returned to the tribe, 78 percent of the 255,000 seriously deteriorated artifacts are preserved and housed in the Tunica-Biloxi Museum.

This 300-year-old Tunica pottery exhibits a pattern closely identified with the Tunica called "Winterville Incised." Coiled and pinched pots made of clay and tempered with crushed clamshells such as this one were made during the Mississippian period, near the time of the arrival of Europeans.

Jean Baptiste Le Moyne de Bienville presented these gifts to Tunica chief Cahura-Joligo to recognize the mutual dependence between the French and the Tunica. Father Pierre François Xavier de Charlevoix said of a visit with Chief Cahura-Joligo in 1721: "Of all the savages of Canada there is none so much depended upon by our commandants as this chief. . . . He trades with the French, whom he supplies with horses and fowls, and he understands his trade very well."

Tunica-Biloxi Museum director Earl Barbry, Jr., stands at a mound on the reservation that predates the tribe's arrival in Marksville. His protection of such mounds stems from respect. "I equate going into a mound to going into a mausoleum, cracking open the vault and lifting the cross and rosary, and even taking the fillings out of someone's teeth," he explains.

In resurfacing the reservation's roads, the tribe still honors the past by paving around a suspected burial site. It is believed that as their ancestors were buried, trees would grow in a circle around the burial site.

In a demonstration of preparations for the annual Fête de Blé, or Corn Feast, a Tunica-Biloxi tribal member shows how parched corn is folded into the corn leaf. The Fête de Blé historically consisted of placing corn on tribal ancestors' graves before dawn to show them honor. The festival continued with a feast of corn, stickball games, and dancing through the night.

Alejos Lopez grew up in Chicago, cut off from his Tunica-Biloxi roots. Upon his retirement he returned to Louisiana to regain his heritage. A self-taught craftsman, Lopez now carves peace pipes and sculptures from pipestone, alabaster, and soapstone.

"EVERYTHING WE DO has to be Indian or we're not Indian anymore. . . . My hope for the tribe is that it survives. Things sometimes fall apart, no matter how great they are. Let the wise solve the problems and keep the greedy out."

Tunica-Biloxi tribal elder Lula Cryer spends most of her time on her farm near Anacoco weaving pine needle baskets and stitching quilts. "I mostly taught myself, and just kept going with it," she says of her basket making skill, which she has passed to her daughter. "Now I can make any kind I want to. You use your imagination and never make two just alike." Born in 1906 and orphaned as a child, Cryer was raised by a white couple. Growing up, she knew she was Indian. "I was always proud to know what I was," she says.

Kayla Johnson's year as Tunica-Biloxi princess deepened her appreciation for a heritage she believes is worth preserving.

"CONSIDERING HOW MANY people there are in the world, there's not that many that are Native American. I feel like I'm one of the lucky few. I feel lucky that there are a lot of people that want to know about our heritage, that I'm one of those people that do know and can teach them. It's not what you look like on the outside. It's what's on the inside."

Native American dancers prepare to enter the dance circle during the Grand Entry of the fourth annual Tunica-Biloxi Pow Wow. Organizer John Barbry is pleased with the impact the pow wow has had on his tribe. "I've seen a lot of my tribal members that have started dancing and singing the old songs," he explains. "Other than our Indian identity, what else can we look to, to bind us together as a community?"

Tribal elder Anna Pierite Juneau sells Indian crafts during the Tunica-Biloxi Pow Wow. Juneau, the daughter of former chief Joseph Pierite, is one of only a handful of elders who still make baskets.

Commemorative T-shirts celebrate the fourth annual Tunica-Biloxi Pow Wow held at the reservation's festival grounds.

Little Princess Taylor Ann Tucker leans against her cousin during the pow wow. Her mother, Crystal Dallmann, says Taylor Ann especially enjoyed performing at the pow wow. "She was very excited, she wanted to know everything. She loved it."

Tribal member Sue Rivas Chavez dances in the women's traditional and buckskin competition at the fourth annual pow wow. Chavez grew up in south Texas. "I was not taught a lot growing up because at the time we were a poor tribe," recalls Chavez. "Children our age are now trying to learn to carry on our traditions, but for whatever reasons, our parents didn't have time to teach."

The Coushatta Tribe of Louisiana

With our victories and accomplishments, we look forward to a better tomorrow. But we must not forget our past, for we have a colorful history that must be remembered for all our children, Indian and non-Indian.
— LOVELIN PONCHO, Chairman of the Coushatta Tribe

TONY BATTISE says quietly, "I'm just going to play the flute, play from my heart." He raises the flute to his mouth, and a strain of endurance and survival drifts hauntingly through the air.

Battise started playing flute when he was twelve. Whether he plays at pow wows, weddings, funerals, or baby christenings, his music is, he says, "a way of expressing myself. A way of story-telling—family history, tribal stories, stories of different things."

The Coushatta are slow to warm to a conversation but quick to reply through their music. While Battise preserves traditions through the notes of a flute, Leland Thompson, with complete self-assurance, picks up a small drum and begins to sing in a high, plaintive voice a song with no words.

"That song was a round dance, a common way of singing and dancing for all the North American tribes. Straight song. No words, just vocals. By the way of the beat and the way it's sung," it would be understood, Thompson said. He performs often at pow wows across the country.

Thompson is cultural consultant for the Coushatta Tribe of Louisiana's social services department. "My job is not only a job, it's something I want to do," he says. "It's preserving our culture for the Coushatta tribe—such things as our language, our customs, our beliefs, our disciplinary sayings—basically everything pertaining to the Coushatta tribe."

Many of today's Coushatta still craft baskets, use medicinal plants to supplement modern medicine, and complement their strong Christian faith with traditional beliefs. Today's Coushatta still speak the language of their ancestors, though fewer than two percent of the state's Native Americans do. Remarkably, of the 175 indigenous languages remaining on the entire continent, only 20 are spoken by people of all ages as vigorously as the Coushatta language. It is spoken in homes and offices and at social gatherings. Younger tribal members who are willing can learn the language from the stories of their elders. With each word, tribal members strengthen the heart of their traditional culture. "Language is first in keeping the culture," says tribal member Rayne Langley. "We're a proud group, not afraid to tell you who we are. A quiet people. Our culture and our language is what we value."

Preserving that culture is a widespread goal among tribal members, Thompson says. The families are the center of this tribe, serving today as cultural consultants to each other much as they have throughout the years. When one family loses a tradition, another family helps them to relearn. We are "very culture based," Thompson explains. Tribal members "don't want to throw their culture and their ideas out to people. They want to keep it to themselves and their family and friends. They want to see their kids not get left behind, but not lose their traditional values."

Though the tribe has managed to keep its culture alive through many centuries, the struggle to sustain its way of life never ends. While many still prefer to keep a distance from the white world, younger members of the tribe are assimilating more and more as they marry nonnative spouses. Battise's aunt, Myrna Wilson, explains how these changes could result in the Coushatta language vanishing in the next generation. "It goes back to the mother, to the parents," she says, "because if the mother speaks only English, it doesn't teach the Coushatta language to the kids. They're losing it right there. I can see that in my grandson because the daddy is nontribal, the mother is Coushatta, and there are few words she speaks to him and he understands."

Wilson's father, Bel Abbey, worked with ethnologists and linguists during his lifetime to create a Coushatta dictionary. Abbey passed down many tribal stories, and worked on a Coushatta translation of the Bible as well. But Coushatta speakers admit they can't easily translate their spoken language into a written version.

"Tribal members cannot understand the phonetic markings that [the linguists] used," Thompson explains. Sharing the Coushatta phrase for "thank you," Thompson and Langley confer about a reasonable way to spell it. They agree that *alcelamo* is fairly close.

"Our language is a household language," Thompson says. "We can communicate to each other. We can understand each other. If somebody outside of the tribe were to listen and understand it, they'd get two variations. They'd probably wonder why the same word was being spoken a little differently. It's just the way the household speaks it. Right now, I'm trying, on my computer, writing it the way it's pronounced. But even that's hard. . . . Different intonation on a word can change meaning from good to great to excellent." Thompson is also working to record the tribe's traditional stories, songs, language, and basket making techniques on audiotapes and videotapes.

For many years, basket making was an essential part of life for the Coushatta tribe. First used within the tribe, the baskets were later currency for tribal members walking house to house, trading baskets for slabs of smoked bacon to feed their families. The traditional Coushatta rivercane and white-oak baskets are no longer made today, but Wilson and other women of the tribe still craft the pine baskets. "My mama used to let us use just the leftover pine needles, whatever she had on the floor," Wilson recalls. The women gathered long-leaf pine needles, bundling them to dry for six weeks. "Then we started making the baskets. We'd sell them or trade them for food or give them as gifts. Whenever I was growing up, the small four-inch baskets were twenty-five cents each. Now, they are forty-five dollars. Here lately, with the casino going on, all the ladies are working. They know how to make them, but it's hard to find time. It's hard to get materials." Long-leaf pine has been replaced by slash pine in many areas, and landowners have been reluctant to allow the tribe access to the remaining long-leaf pine trees. These days, vendors bring in boxes full of bundled long-leaf needles from northern Louisiana.

Elders tell Thompson they worry that the young people of the tribe are more interested in sports, video games, and television than they are in carrying on tribal traditions. He recognizes it is difficult but believes it is possible to honor traditional ways while living in a modern world. "There shouldn't be a giving up of one for the other," says the twenty-three-year-old Thompson, who spoke only Coushatta until learning English in the first grade. "They can be combined."

Thompson recalls being taught disciplinary sayings about proper ways to behave, including how to treat others and the natural world. He never learned the specific reasons for their importance, but adhered to many during his wife's first pregnancy. Watching movies with violent content and walking across wires, for instance, was prohibited. "Our elders told us what we can't do, but they wouldn't tell us why. And then I started going back and asking, and they said, 'Well, it's just a discipline.' Questioning an elder would be questioning an authority figure, so it would be disrespectful. But I explained to them why we need to know, because so many of the reasons are being lost."

Whether or not the reasons are clear, Thompson, like most of the tribal members, still honors the tribe's traditions. When his daughter, Gwyneth, was four months old, the family held a predawn hair shaving ceremony. "It's the last rite of cleansing from the mother's womb," he explains. The baby's hair is "the last part of the mother on the child," and the ceremony is "the time you decide what you want your baby to be interested in. Whatever you think will help your baby in the future is placed under the child, and it's also a gift to the child."

Thompson placed under Gwyneth a Bible, a dictionary and a river-cane basket he had just learned to make. Other gifts included eagle feathers for dancing. Though tradition holds that the child's uncle should perform the shaving, Gwyneth has no uncles. His grandmother shaved Gwyneth, just as she had shaved Leland when he was four months old but had no uncles. "The hair is taken up and kept," he says. "It came from the baby. You put it somewhere in your house. You can't throw it away because the baby still needs it. In its own way, it gets lost. It makes its way out."

Thompson confesses that in his efforts to preserve the tribe's traditions, it takes time for him to convince elders to share information that they have spent a lifetime honoring as sacred. "I go to each elder, sit with them, visit with them, because they're not open to just anybody. Some of them don't really know me yet. They know of me but they don't know how I really function, how I take in their information. So I go sit down and visit with them and talk about things like the weather, how their week's been going. After a few visits, they start getting comfortable, and then I start talking to them about what kind of information I'm looking for, and if it's all right to get that information from them. If not, I stay away from it and go on to another subject. They ask me who I am, what my name is, who my father and mother are. They ask me what clan I am. After that, some of them right off the bat are pretty open. Some of them aren't too comfortable. I'm almost like a stranger," he says.

Thompson is half Coushatta and half Alabama-Coushatta. The Alabama and Coushatta tribes have been closely associated throughout their history. Both were members of the Creek Confederacy and are of Muskhogean language stock. Originally located in Mississippi, Alabama, and Georgia, both tribes underwent long journeys of more than one hundred years to reach their new homes. The Alabama-Coushatta tribe formed as members of both tribes eventually settled near Livingston, Texas. The Coushatta Tribe of Louisiana, traditionally known as Koasati, settled in the Elton and Kinder areas of Louisiana.

The Coushatta tribe's recorded history dates back to 1540, when Hernando de Soto and his men kidnapped their chief and other tribal members, threatening to burn them alive if they resisted future attacks. De Soto was in search of gold, though the Coushatta knew there was none in the area. Gold was a meaningless metal to the primarily agricultural tribe, which lived near the Tennessee River.

The Coushatta made it through the seventeenth century on fairly peaceful terms with the French, Spanish, and English settlers. The fledgling United States government, however, encouraged settlers to move farther into Indian country, claiming Indian lands for themselves. In 1783 the Coushatta tribe lost more than eight hundred square miles of their territory in a treaty with the State of Georgia. This was one in a series of treaties, agreements, and confrontations that forced the tribe from its traditional home. Among the confrontations was the Creek War of 1813–1814, in which more than 3,000 warriors were killed and twenty-two million acres of land was lost.

The group walked across Georgia, Alabama, and Mississippi before a Coushatta leader named Red Shoes led a small contingent of eighty to one hundred people into Louisiana, settling along the southern reaches of the Red River. Hundreds more followed, and they reestablished their political and social system, enabling them to preserve their traditional way of life despite further forced moves within Louisiana. The basic social tie of the Coushatta remains the family unit, or clan.

By 1861, the tribe was living along the Calcasieu River near Kinder. As land-hungry settlers forged into that area, the tribe purchased land near Elton in Allen Parish, and most moved there in 1884. Tribal members live in both locations today, continuing to follow their matriarchal clan system. "The clans were family units among the tribe to keep intermarriages from happening," explains Thompson. "It was a society structure too, and each clan had its own head speaker who in turn worked with the chief." The seven large clans still in existence are those of the Deer, the Panther, the Beaver, the Daddy Long Legs spider, the Bear, the Turkey, and the Bobcat.

Federal recognition first came in 1868, when 160 acres of land was placed in trust for the tribe. Federal educational and medical assistance programs arrived by 1930, including an elementary school, but in 1953 the Bureau of Indian Affairs' termination policy halted services to the tribe and removed the land from trust. Legally this meant the Coushatta tribe no longer officially existed.

In 1965, members of the tribe formed the Coushatta Indians of Allen Parish, Inc., a tribal arts and crafts business. They made baskets and other crafts, sold them to the business and in turn, they were sold to the public. "That was their living," recalls tribal elder Florine Pitre. "They had lost their services. It was a way of raising money." This venture also provided a gathering place for tribal members, and in so doing laid the groundwork for the push to regain recognition.

Coushatta members appealed to the Louisiana state legislature for recognition, receiving it in 1972. The same year, federal officials agreed to resume providing contract medical services to the tribe. The tribe then formed Coushatta Alliance, Inc., which drafted a tribal constitution and sought funding for governmental development and a tribal office. The federal government formally recognized the Coushatta Tribe of Louisiana as a sovereign nation on June 27, 1973. Two years later, federal proclamation designated fifteen acres of land as the tribal reservation. It took two hundred years, but the Coushatta are once again rooted to an area by soil. The tribe now has approximately one thousand acres in trust and owns a total of three thousand acres to be used for investment purposes.

"There are so many things you can do with land," says tribal chairman Lovelin Poncho. The success of the Grand Casino Coushatta, opened in 1995, allowed the Coushatta to purchase land for rice, soybean, and crawfish farming, as well as horse and cattle ranching. The Coushatta also hope to start a timber business with a solid wildlife management program.

With the welcome new capital, tribal members upgraded their homes from substandard dwellings needing extensive repairs to modern, well-constructed houses. A neighborhood of small, neatly maintained HUD-subsidized homes can be seen from the cluster of administrative buildings that house the tribal office, the cultural center, and educational center. The social services office and tribal court are across the street, near the construction site for the tribe's first permanent fire and police station.

Gaming has provided opportunities for tribal members to pursue higher education, improve their health care, secure services for their aging family members, and consider other options for economic development. The casino's success has also enabled the Coushatta to invest more resources in efforts to preserve their heritage. This investment is crucial to the tribe, since the casino's opening also propelled many tribal members into the "white man's world."

"People were afraid that with the casino opening, we might start losing our culture," recalls Langley. "We weren't going to take chances on that happening. That's how the camp started. We wanted to keep the culture, so we started teaching the kids and then have them teach the nontribal people. . . . It's working the way we wanted it to." Camp Coushatta, the tribe's nationally recognized venue for bolstering the tribe's culture among its younger members, allows more than fifty tribal youngsters to share their culture with non-Indians every year. Each day of the camp's six-week summer session, different nonprofit groups bring children to experience Indian culture. Up to two thousand children attend the summer camp program each year, and children also come to four-day camps during the school year to learn more about the tribe and Native American history.

Camp Coushatta's headquarters include a new log-cabin meeting area and museum in a field surrounded by woods. Campers find sixteen learning stations along trails in the circle of piney woods, and a clearing in the midst of the circle exhibits a teepee village reminiscent of a Plains Indian settlement. At the stations, young people learn drumming, singing, dancing, traditional basket making, and jewelry making. The tribal youth learn to throw a tomahawk and spear and to cook the fry bread that sustained tribal members for generations, and they learn the difference between the traditional Coushatta palmetto huts and the teepees of the Plains Indians.

Tribal attorney Randy Doucet says maintaining the culture is critical. "The greatest asset of the tribe is their history, their culture. That's what makes you a tribe and gives you the ability to claim sovereignty," the tribal member says. "It's important to preserve our history and our culture. Once you lose it, it's easy for people to start tearing down your sovereignty. We've got to maintain our distinction, and yet at the same time be good citizens of the state and the United States."

Camp Coushatta does more than help sustain tribal culture. Once the youngsters learn the information and are trained to present it, they overcome their initial shyness. Their newfound speaking abilities have followed them back to school each fall, aiding them in their schoolwork. Langley, the tribe's arts coordinator, says the camp also instills a stronger work ethic and sense of responsibility in the tribe's youth. When the tribe first opened the casino, members worried that some might depend too heavily on their per-capita distributions. "The camp helps train people, shows them how to work," Langley says. "We pay them a stipend, and we made a bank for them here so they could learn about saving and money management."

Tribal Education Director Shirley Doucet believes the camp has been an effective tool in her fight to keep the tribe's children in school. "Camp Coushatta has been a tremendous help. It encourages students to stay in school, get a good education, keep their attendance up, and gives them a respect for authority," Doucet explains. "There's a lot of confidence and self-esteem now." Former camper Chrystal Bertrand, nineteen, is a good example. "I liked the responsibility of the camp. I felt older, proud, because I had a job," she remembers. "It was very interesting, too. This is where I learned about my culture."

Bertrand, who performed the Fancy Dance when she was younger, still announces the dance portions of the camp. Langley says the dance demonstrations have proven popular. "Before, there was no kind of dancing going on," Langley says. "Just a few would go out dancing in the pow wow world. Now, since we started this camp, there's more dancing. We had maybe two when we first started; now we're up to about ten dancers. They pretty much learn on their own, going to different pow wows and seeing other people dance. They go home, play their Indian tape, and they just dance to it 'til they learn on their own."

Langley, who's partial to the music of bands like Alice in Chains and Soundgarden, has no difficulty balancing the traditional with the modern. While he spends his days cultivating the tribe's rich heritage, he spends his free time creating his own music, either as lead singer in an alternative rock band or in his home recording studio. He even hopes to bring his creative talents to fruit with a horror film some day.

In the interim, Langley hopes that programs will continue to include activities to keep youngsters out of trouble. The tribe now organizes at least six youth clubs, in addition to choral and music classes. Through the clubs, such as Y-NOT (Young Natives of Today) and YES (Young Eager Spirits), the social services staff works to teach the youth life lessons, Thompson explains.

For Lovelin Poncho, tribal chairman for the past twelve years, life lessons came in another country. He says the time he spent in the military helped him to stay on the right path. "In the long run, I really gained some experience about what life is all about. If not for the military, I probably would have ended up on the streets or in jail," divulges the man who now leads his tribe. Growing up, Poncho spent his time hunting, fishing, and pitching in with woodcutting, clothes washing, and cooking duties while his parents migrated from job to job. He remembers visiting with other tribes to play stickball when he was young. The Vietnam veteran says his military years were difficult, as combat in Da Nang was a far cry from his sheltered home environment. His experience taught him that the most pressing issue for his people is education. Under Poncho's leadership, the tribe works continually to improve the education level of its children.

Tribal intervention in education starts early. Between tribal homes on Bobcat Clan Lane sits the tribal preschool, which gives children a grounding in the Coushatta language. Once the children are in public or private schools, casino revenues allow the tribe to cover the costs of extracurricular activities such as sports and field trips. The tribe provides incentives for good grades and attendance to its schoolchildren. Grand Casino Coushatta offers tutors to help dropouts get their high school graduation equivalency diploma. A satellite program from McNeese State University offers college courses at the casino as well. For those who wish to attend college, the tribe pays their costs.

"Our young people have so much now it's unbelievable, and yet they don't know what to do with it," says tribal elder Barbara Langley. "When I see the young people with so much opportunity—because of the per-capita they feel like they don't need school anymore. But it won't go on like this. It's really messing up our young children. I think some of the young people are wasting the money, wasting their lives away. We need to teach them values, but I don't think they are willing to learn. They don't have time to talk to the elders. The cultural program is trying to help with the younger ones."

As Chairman Poncho says, it lies with the parents to teach their children. Tony Battise recognizes his responsibility for his own infant son. "I want him to grow up and be educated, know everything he wants to know and not to lose his language and his culture—to know where he comes from and where his people come from," Battise explains. "As long as he grows up to be a good person, that's all I want for him. I'll teach him as he grows up when he wants to learn, what he wants to learn. If he asks me more, then I'll teach him more. For right now I'll teach him our language and our culture and things that I was taught by Mother and Grandfather and everyone around me."

Jackson Langley holds Monroe Langley in this photograph that hangs in the Coushatta Museum. Jackson was born in 1870 in Indian Village, near the Calcasieu River west of Kinder. Like many Coushatta in the late 1800s, Langley worked in a sawmill in Indian Village. (Courtesy Coushatta Museum.)

A self-taught flutist, tribal member Tony Battise plays from his heart. "I was born to be a unique person," Battise explains, "because we are a different nationality of people. I'm proud to be who I am and what I am and to be part of the tribe."

Leland Thompson sings a traditional Coushatta song while taping for a radio program called *Oyate Ta Olowan*, or *The Songs of the People*.

"IT JUST MAKES me feel good to sing and dance, for other people to enjoy it also. They're dancing, they have their shoulders back, they have their head high, they're proud, they're happy. This makes us all one. This makes us a happy people. All the songs—southern style, northern style—it comes together. It just makes everybody feel good about themselves, who they are. They're not ashamed they're Native American. They're not ashamed they're not the same tribe as another person. It becomes a common ground for everybody."

Coushatta tribal member Steven Robinson begins to make traditional corn soup called *sofkee* outside his grandfather's home near Elton. Robinson adds what he describes as "homemade ingredients taught to him by his grandfather" as he boils the corn for three hours in a large, black kettle. Despite the hard work it takes to prepare the soup, Robinson is glad he learned how to make it: "I learned from my grandpa and plus, they depend on you to make it whenever they want it."

To prepare the corn for the *sofkee*, Robinson pounds whole dried corn until it can be sifted through two baskets with progressively tighter weaves.

Tribal member Madeline Celestine sews the top of a coiled pine needle basket at her home near Elton. Longleaf pine is native to the area, and Celestine is one of many tribal members who bind these needles with raffia to fashion detailed effigies of animals and a variety of useful baskets. Celestine, who has made pine needle baskets for 60 years, learned the craft from her mother when she was a little girl.

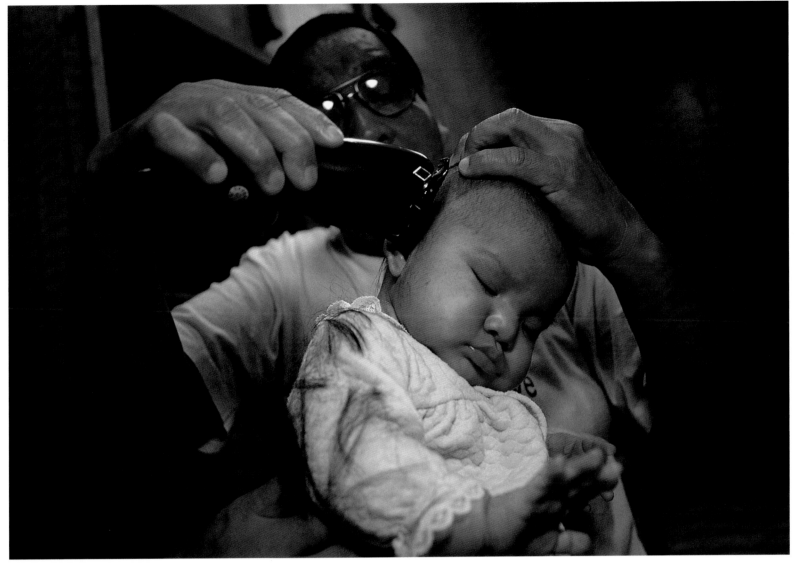

Gideon Robinson shaves the hair from the head of his four-month-old great niece, Kaylyn Poncho, at the Indian Bible Church near the Coushatta reservation. A Bible is underneath the baby to signify spiritual growth. It is Coushatta tradition for an uncle to shave a baby's head before sunrise when the child reaches the age of four months. The shaving represents a new beginning—a way to cleanse the child and to take sickness away. Kaylyn's grandmother, Melissa Battise, insisted that everyone in the family wake up before sunrise to participate. "I don't want to lose this tradition. It's like keeping our language," she says.

Tribal chairman Lovelin Poncho sits in the tribe's new museum with artwork of the tribe's seven matriarchal clans behind him. In early Coushatta culture, at least twelve clans, each symbolized by a particular animal or element, were part of the social organization of the tribe. Poncho was born into the Turkey clan at his grandmother's one-room house near Bayou Blue in Allen Parish in 1947. Elected chairman in 1987, Poncho has seen his tribe reach its goal of economic independence and self-sufficiency.

Chairman Lovelin Poncho recognizes the debt the Coushatta owe to elders like Solomon Battise, above, for their role in cultural preservation. Battise is one of the tribe's last river cane basket makers. Poncho's staff takes pains to organize social gatherings, field trips, meals, and medical care for the tribe's oldest members. "The elderly are important," he says. "We need to take care of them because they are the ones who took care of our culture. They did a tremendous job of keeping our heritage together all these years."

Grand Casino Coushatta opened in January 1995 and has greatly enhanced opportunities for Coushatta tribal members. The second largest employer in Allen Parish, the casino has over 170,000 square feet of gaming area and is adjoined by a 233-room hotel and a 200-pad RV park. Casino revenues have greatly improved tribal housing and have funded a new tribal medical center, improved infrastructure, and many educational programs.

83

Youth rodeo and trail rides are popular among the Coushatta, but for Hilton Langley and his son Attrail Langley, this was their first ride around the Coushatta reservation with their new horse Skeeter. Hilton says he used to ride years ago but only recently bought the horse because his three children were fascinated with the horses they saw around the reservation.

Since the U.S. government officially recognized the tribe as a sovereign nation in 1973, the tribe has increased its land in trust to more than 1,000 acres. The tribe has developed a housing improvement program, using much of this land to construct new homes.

Monica Langley dribbles on the basketball court at the Coushatta Multipurpose Complex. In the foreground is the Coushatta tribal logo, which was designed in the late 1970s as the tribe reorganized during the federal recognition process. The garfish in the center of the logo represents wisdom, courage, and discipline. Historically, the garfish was a main food staple of the Coushatta and was also used for jewelry and medicine. The five colors in the logo—red, orange, black, yellow, and white—represent life-giving blood, discipline, night, sunrise, and day.

The success of Grand Casino Coushatta has enabled the Coushatta tribe to build new facilities for administrative and tribal services such as the Social Services Department building, shown here. The Social Services Department building is adjacent to the Coushatta Multipurpose Complex. This new complex includes a full-sized gymnasium, an exercise room, a sauna and steam area, and a recreational area.

Coushatta Police officers Terrell John (left) and T. A. Wier stand beside their vehicle on a gravel road near the reservation in Allen Parish. "My goal is to have more interaction with the community, especially young people under the age of 20. I want to get to know them better. Working in a big city, you don't get to know as many people," says Officer Wier.

Tribal member Garrett Nichols watches his sister run barrels during a practice session at the Coushatta Ranch in Sulphur. The 32-acre ranch, with state-of-the-art facilities and a horse-breeding program for tribal members, provides hands-on experience with horsemanship, fishing, canoeing, and other outdoor activities.

As a sovereign Indian nation, the Coushatta tribe makes its own laws. Court Clerk Michelle Litteral is pictured here with Judge Randy Doucet in the Coushatta courtroom. Doucet has since become the tribal attorney and works to protect the tribe's sovereign status.

"OUR ANCESTORS MADE a deal. Tribes ceded everything, keeping only a small portion of their lands, with the understanding that tribes would be allowed to live the way they had been living. It's a never-ending struggle for tribes throughout the United States to maintain their sovereignty. There are people who are bitterly opposed to tribal sovereignty. It's important for the United States to maintain its treaties and agreements with the Indians tribes, just as the United States wants other countries to abide by their treaties and agreements, no matter how old."

—RANDY DOUCET

For many visitors, the best part of the Camp Coushatta experience is to taste Indian fry bread prepared by Coushatta youth in the kitchen of the tribe's new museum. In times past, the bread was the mainstay of the Coushatta diet.

Pine needle baskets on display at the Coushatta Museum.

Responding to the applause of the audience, Randy Santiago dances enthusiastically to the beat of the drum at Camp Coushatta.

Tribal members Boyd Langley (left) and Randy Santiago wait their turn to perform fancy dance at Camp Coushatta. The tribal youth teach Native American crafts and traditions at the camp to nearly two thousand visitors each year.

In a typically cluttered teenager's room, Raynella Thompson prepares for her high school prom. After a limousine ride to Lake Charles for dinner, Thompson and her date will spend the entire night at Elton High School's alcohol-free prom.

"I HOPE THAT ONE DAY the younger generation realize you need an education to better your life, to find a decent job that you can work your way up. We have a lot of problems with alcoholism, drug abuse, high school dropouts. I hope there comes a time when they realize they need to achieve more for themselves and as a community."

At the Elton High School prom, Aletha Langley slow dances with Wilber Istre. Langley paired up with tribal member Raynella Thompson and her date to attend Elton High School's overnight alcohol-free prom.

Proud parents Sanford and Ethel Robinson receive a rose and a hug from their high school daughter Jill at her 1999 graduation from Elton High School. An outstanding high school basketball player, Jill is now a student at McNeese State University.

With the assistance of tribal funding, Derek Poncho and Rebecca Breaux attend Louisiana State University in Baton Rouge. Breaux is in her first semester, and Poncho is majoring in electrical engineering. "I want to get out and make something for myself and not rely on the revenue from the casino," says Poncho. Poncho's father, Dinaray Poncho, was the first Coushatta to graduate from college.

93

Mixing his love for music with his love for movie production, tribal member Rayne Langley spends many hours at a sound-board. "I love the feeling of creating something from nothing, whether it's music, a script for a movie, or even just a drawing," he says. Langley is the arts coordinator for the tribe's Social Services Department and is the lead singer in a local rock band.

Tribal member Winston John plays with the Zydeco Night Riders at a party near Kinder. John grew up listening to Elvis Presley and started playing guitar when he was 12 but didn't begin performing with a band until he was 45. He was at an Indian Days festival at the reservation when he was recruited to play with the members of his current band.

Barry Langley, a self-described advocate for native people, at the New Orleans Jazz and Heritage Festival.

"I'M AN ACTIVIST because as an ethnic group we're misunderstood. There are a lot of half-truths and a lot of stereotypes. I remember giving a speech at a high school in Baton Rouge. . . . I asked how many people expected to see me in an Indian outfit with feathers. The majority raised their hands. . . . People are aware that we're out there, we have a rich history, but times change, people change. . . . People should understand that the majority of Indians are not noble savages, not the Indians in the John Wayne movies. We are a passive people. Like anyone else we tried to protect our territory, our people, our way of life. What other ethnic group maintains their ways after so much time?"

Jerome Poncho prepares to carry the American flag during the Grand Entry of the Coushatta Pow Wow. A veteran of World War II, Poncho served as an Army Air Corps aircraft mechanic for P-51 Mustangs. Before and after his military service, Poncho worked wherever he could around what he calls "Indian country."

"THE INDIANS HAD a hard time getting hired. . . . I've seen rougher days, so I hope the younger generation can improve their education and buy more property for themselves so they can have a better life, for them and for their families."

Tribal member Joey Poncho waits in the van as his parents, Janson and Danielle, finish with their regalia for the start of a pow wow. Joey started going to pow wows when he was three months old and won in his first tiny tot grass dancer contest at the Alabama-Coushatta Pow Wow in Livingston, Texas. Not all Coushatta children participate in pow wows, but Joey's father says the pow wow circle teaches discipline and respect and Joey can learn a lot from the elders who participate.

With her colorful fringes swirling around her, tribal member Tracy Poncho energetically dances in the women's fancy shawl competition at the Tunica-Biloxi Pow Wow. Although this dance requires more motion and agility than most dances, the woman's grace is always expressed in the fancy shawl.

Tribal members enjoy a basketball game at dusk on the Coushatta reservation.

Little Indian School students (from left) Destiny Crosby, Kabrina Robinson, and Elaina Langley concentrate on a preschool computer program.

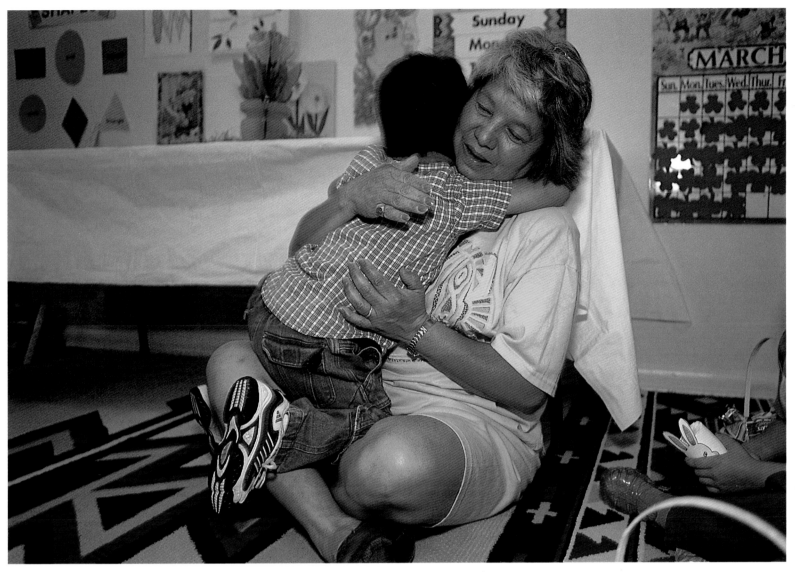

Hugs are just as important as numbers and letters at the Little Indian School. Tribal elder Barbara Langley, founder of the school, teaches preschoolers about life and love.

"EVEN BEFORE RECOGNITION, growing up as a little girl, I remember our grandparents taught us a lot about our duty. We didn't have newspapers, magazines, or TV. We spent time together talking about things, and they set the standards for us to follow. . . . We had a close-knit family. We didn't have anything. We were poor, but we had a loving family and that was a lot. . . . We've lost our close-knit families in the tribe. I'd like to see that back, that working together to help each other. Only when we can do that can we move forward."

The Jena Band of Choctaw Indians

The Choctaw have taken care of themselves for a long time. We draw strength from our culture.
—CLYDE JACKSON, former chairman of the Jena Band of Choctaw Indians, 1976
testimony to American Indian Policy Review Commission

IN 1880, census records showed twenty-six Indians living in four households near the small town of Jena, Louisiana. They should have been in Oklahoma, like the thousands of other Choctaw forcibly removed from Mississippi. But their ancestors followed Indian hunting trails and colonial routes west instead, beyond Catahoula Lake to a small stream in the remote central Louisiana pine forests. Exactly why they settled along Trout Creek remains a mystery. Perhaps it was the abundant wildlife surrounding Catahoula Lake, whose name is derived from the Choctaw *okhata hullo*, meaning "beloved lake." Or perhaps it was the isolation of the sparsely populated farming community.

Jerry Jackson, who for years researched the tribe's history, relates that once there, the forebears of the Jena Band of Choctaw Indians eked out a living as sharecroppers. They survived by working the nearby cotton fields and cattle pastures of the Whatley farm in return for credit at the company store.

At the beginning of the twentieth century a new federal law offered the Jena band a chance to reunite with its Choctaw brethren. The Dawes Commission sought to identify Indians lost during the relocation of their tribes to the Indian Territory. If the Jena band could prove its Choctaw ancestry to the commission, members would be eligible for their own land in Oklahoma. With little to lose, many of the tribal members walked the hundreds of miles to Muskogee, Oklahoma, to testify. Jackson explains that they decided to undertake the arduous nine-month journey as a result of "years and years and years, decades, of working and not having nothing." Knowing they were full-blooded Choctaw, the group counted on becoming members of the more established Oklahoma Choctaw Nation.

Tribal elder Mary Jackson Jones, respectfully referred to as "Miss Mary," says she heard her mother and father discussing the trip many times. "They wanted to go there because they were promised land and a better life. They went up there. There was nothing there for them," she relates softly, adding that the trip taught the tribe not to trust outsiders. "It was hard time for them to get back. Some of them didn't make it back."

Upon returning in March 1903, they learned their testimony had qualified them for land allotments—provided they return to Oklahoma by August. It was an impossible journey to make in five months. Exhausted and disheartened, the Jena band withdrew to its settlement near the quiet waters of Trout Creek. Some of band's five families would later move, joining other Choctaw-speaking Indians in Oklahoma. In the ensuing years, another Choctaw family—the Lewises—arrived to help keep the small group viable. Its nomadic days over, the Jena band isolated itself in Eden, Louisiana. Separated from the much larger Oklahoma and Mississippi Choctaw nations, this handful of families endured into the next millennium to become a sovereign nation.

Today, all that remains of the Jena band's original Trout Creek settlement area is the burial ground. The cemetery can be found down a dusty logging road, hidden in an area the Jena band's ancestors inhabited long ago. Trees that once wrapped around Whiterock Cemetery have been clear-cut. The logging work does not cross the chain link fence, however, and the Indian cemetery remains peaceful. Perhaps forty graves, well maintained and mostly marked with wooden crosses, lie in the silence. "The cemetery has always been sacred to the tribe," says tribal member Clyde Jackson. Landowners donated the site to the tribe, whose members worked their fields. "It lifted everybody's spirits to have the land. We knew nobody would disturb it once it was ours."

Like the eternal pull of the moon on the tide, the tribe's members have been drawn to the cemetery from the time they were first buried there. They come together regularly to keep the burial ground clean, toting lawn chairs, lawn mowers, and refreshments in preparation for the day's work. They clear weeds near the teddy bear, miniature cars, and toy ninja turtle resting upon an infant's grave. They cut grass around the flowers perched in worn leather boots stationed at attention at either side of the headstone of Elmer Lewis, a Korean War and Vietnam veteran who died in 1995. "To me when I get there, it feels like my home. I feel free," Miss Mary says.

Rocks of different shapes and sizes can be found on many of the graves, placed there lovingly by family members like Miss Mary. "I find some pretty rocks and put them on Mama and

Daddy's graves," she says. "I don't believe in just picking up anything without giving Mother Earth any thank you. I teach my children that. You offer something. Once I found a beautiful heart-shaped white rock. It was big and pretty. I had nothing to offer, but I wanted it. So I took three or four pieces of my hair and gave it. I got that rock and put it on my mama's grave, and it is still there."

Tribal members speak of their ancestors with reverence for good reason. Beginning with the walk from Mississippi and through the trek to Oklahoma and all the years they toiled as tenant farmers, these native people kept the tribe alive. The tribe sustained its distinct culture even as Anglo, French, Spanish, and Irish immigrants populated the land around them. That is something today's tribal leaders do not forget.

"We stayed to ourselves, we kept our traditions, we kept our customs," Chief B. Cheryl Smith explains. While Smith's appreciation of those who preserved the tribe's old ways is heartfelt, her appearance is that of a modern businesswoman. Her genuine warmth, however, quickly makes visitors feel welcome. "We kept our leadership; there was a person who handled problems, who handled burials. We maintained," she continues. "That's how we were able to get recognition. We were able to preserve, able to survive."

Smith's mother, Miss Mary, can remember tribal leaders conducting those ceremonies. "The traditional funeral, when they bury the person that dies, they all leave and go back home," she explains. Women then wore black during a six-week mourning period, while the men of the tribe didn't shave or cut their hair. "When those six weeks was over, they all go back to the cemetery and have the funeral all over again." The second funeral, literally called a "cry over again" in the Choctaw language, signaled the end of the mourning period.

Miss Mary says the tribe's children still laugh when she tells them of traditional weddings. To determine whether the boy and girl were ready for marriage, a race was held. The girl had to run as fast as she could to a line, and the boy had to catch her before she reached the line. If she ran too slowly, or the boy could not catch her, they had to wait another year before the chief would perform the wedding. "Nobody draws lines anymore," Miss Mary says with a smile. "Nobody runs anymore. They stand still and spend a lot of money."

Through the 1930s, '40s, and '50s, the Jena band couldn't stand still. They began to hunt for better job opportunities, many times on foot. Some traveled the forty-odd miles to Alexandria to work in a charcoal factory. Others spread into the woods, cutting logs and pulpwood or blowing up pine stumps for the Alexandria Pine Knot Company. Some worked in the Trout sawmill. Some farmed. Many of the women took in ironing and hired out as housekeepers. "Poverty was there, but I don't think they realized they were in poverty," explains former chief Clyde Jackson. He attributes the poor economic situation directly to the fact that Indians were barred from public schools until the 1940s. "They struggled; they didn't have a whole lot. They couldn't get jobs that required any education at all."

Trying to gain a foothold on a more stable economic path, tribal members met in 1974 and decided to take the road to federal recognition. "We thought that in a short while we'd be federally recognized and they would have houses and medical benefits. They thought, just looking around the room, 'Well, there can't be anybody more Indian than we are,'" remembers Jerry Jackson.

The tribe started moving toward recognition by electing officials and formally incorporating as the Jena Band of Choctaw Indians. They then began diligently gathering the mind-boggling array of information required by the Bureau of Indian Affairs. Their petition had to prove the

Jena band met seven specific criteria, including Indian descendancy, continual leadership, existence as a distinct community, and established relationships with the federal government.

Without experience navigating the bureaucratic maze, the tribe took ten years to submit its first round of applications to the Bureau of Indian Affairs. Once there, it was quickly buried beneath piles of other petitions waiting in line for the agency's attention. According to the bureau, of the 150 petitions for federal recognition it had received since 1978, only 12 had received recognition through the process by the end of the century.

Tribal council member and former chief Jerry Jackson explains, "In 1986, when I came on board, we were pretty much stymied. . . . We were like 103, 104 on the [bureau's] list." Given an estimate of fifteen years before their application would be reviewed, Jackson began to seek out legislators in hopes of finding another path to recognition. Three different times, the tribe fought to push a bill through the House and Senate for recognition before the bill finally reached the desk of President George Bush. Acceding to the Bureau of Indian Affairs' opinion that the legislation would allow other tribes to bypass the formal recognition process, Bush pocket-vetoed the measure.

Meanwhile, the Jena band hired genealogical experts to assist in the petition's documentation. Digging through Dawes Commission testimony, they discovered the link to their past that served as a starting point in tracing the tribe's Indian descendancy. The report revealed their ancestors had come from Mississippi during the Choctaw removal. The removal period began in 1830, when the Treaty of Dancing Rabbit Creek mandated the evacuation of all Choctaw from their remaining thirty-six million acres to reservations in what was to become Oklahoma. The treaty followed the Indian Removal Act, in which Congress called for the relocation of the southeastern tribes, including the Choctaw, Cherokee, Creek, Chickasaw, and Seminole peoples. This forced migration came to be known as the Trail of Tears.

Armed with additional documentation, Jerry Jackson continued to exert political pressure despite the veto. Finally they hammered out a compromise. The Jena band agreed not to bring its bill back to Congress, and in exchange the BIA agreed to review its petition. "Once they got to looking at our case and at our documents, there was no question," Jackson says. "But it was trying to get in position to get somebody to look at you—you had to use the politics, you had to use whatever forces to make the staff see it."

After twenty-one years of traveling down first one path then another, the Jena finally reached their destination. The federal government granted the Jena Band of Choctaw Indians federal recognition in 1995. Nearly eighty years after the first tribe in Louisiana was federally recognized, the Jena became the fourth and last to have their status as a sovereign nation affirmed in the twentieth century. "It was such a big deal, to wait for it all your life," Cheryl Smith remembers.

Yet the Jena band's elation soon dissipated. The initial funding the BIA disbursed upon recognition did little to cover the cost of administrating tribal services. Though welcome, their newly recognized status did not move the Jena band out of poverty. It took another full year to identify new funding sources to address the most pressing housing and health-care needs. "In some aspects a lot of people were disappointed, but there were a lot of people out there that were just thankful that we got [recognition]," Smith remembers. "I didn't think it was something I'd see in my lifetime. It's the biggest accomplishment the tribe's ever done, and will have ever done."

Smith, one of the original participants in the drive for federal recognition, says the tribe has expanded many programs and created a number of jobs since 1995. In her second term as chief, she is still striving earnestly to make improvements for her people, such as using health-care grants to provide free preventive medical care, eye care, dental care, and prescription drug coverage. Recognition has also enabled tribal administration to implement education, housing, and cultural programs for its 234 members. "We're able to do things now that we never were before. Our services aren't great, but still they're more than we've ever had before," she says.

Tribal council member Christine Norris has felt the impact on the health-care programs that she administers. "We have been able to expand a little bit, to provide diabetes screenings," Norris explains. "Economic development would help us to service those people who are in our tribe but not in our service area." Nearly 40 percent of the tribe's members are diabetic. Nationally, Indians suffer a death rate from diabetes that is 249 percent higher than all other races in the country.

Though health care is her first priority, Norris adds that the tribal council is intent on raising the educational level of the tribe so members can find better employment opportunities. An incentive program pays children for the A's and B's they earn on their report cards. "We have a party for everyone who graduates from high school at the tribal center and give each graduate a hundred dollars," says Norris. "We have more in college than ever before."

Norris' excitement is understandable. Public education was not available to Indians through the mid-twentieth century. Former chief Bill Lewis, with the help of the La Salle Parish school superintendent, started the first class for Choctaw children at the Eden Methodist Church in 1930. It closed the following year. The Penick Indian School opened three years later, lasting five years before running out of funds. It wasn't until after World War II that Indians really started going to public schools, and it wasn't until 1964 that a tribal member actually graduated from high school.

But along with the need to relocate to find jobs, tribal members' increased access to education has had a downside. Norris remembers growing up in the late twentieth century, when the tribe's customs were beginning to fade and fewer people were speaking the language: "We did not have a reservation, did not all live together; we were all scattered out and felt like we'd become part of the white system up here. I hate to say that word. We were raised up all going to white schools, never went to Indian schools. We've been immersed into the mainstream of society along with everybody else, and it's taken away the cultural aspect for our youth."

As they realized the fabric of their culture was beginning to fray, the Jena band began to place more of a focus on helping their children understand their heritage. "Since [gaining federal] recognition we've been able to make an impact," Smith explains. "When I was in school, we didn't focus on our Indianness. Now we have Indian tutoring and language programs and facilities to get us together."

The Jena band's new multipurpose center aims to be the nucleus of the tribe, with large spaces for social gatherings, meetings, and sporting events. As Miss Mary blessed the opening of the tribal center, she fanned burning sage toward the enlarged tribal logo, which depicts an Indian family in the midst of a journey. She prayed in Choctaw for the ancestors who worked so hard to keep the tribe together on their most recent journey, and she expressed similar thoughts later in English. "A lot of our people wait for this, now they done gone. But I know they here today. It's just a feeling, a presence of their spirit," she shares.

One has a sense of going back to another time when meeting Miss Mary, a former council member who can speak to the past and future of her tribe with eloquence in both her native language and English. Many of her thoughts expressed in English retain a soft, lilting Choctaw cadence. Miss Mary serves the Jena band in many ways. Often, members of the tribe come to her for help. She listens patiently to their problems, offering wise words of advice. She sees her ability to assist as something she must cherish. "A lot of the Indian people have this but they don't know what to do with it," she offers. "They're scared. They have the spirit but they're scared. My own people, they could be doing real good. But they're scared."

The evidence of years of experience is sculpted into the face of this full-blooded Choctaw elder who wears her long silver-streaked hair in a braid flowing down her back. She fashions necklaces from chinaberries dyed into varied hues and weaves ribbon shirts coveted by singers and musicians of other tribes.

Tribal members like Clyde Jackson join Miss Mary in keeping the tribe's traditions alive. He spends hours scraping, rubbing, and soaking deer hides in the painstakingly slow Choctaw tanning process, much as his sharecropper forebears did to pay for goods in a different time. His son is interested in learning the art, and Jackson is pleased. "I do the traditional hide tanning and now I'm trying to teach the Choctaw language," he says. "That's two traditions I'd like to keep going."

Probably nobody under forty speaks the language, admits Smith, who was once fluent. Now, she can only understand the language, not speak it. Her mother is one of fewer than a dozen tribal members who are still fluent. "Linguists have told us that our Choctaw language is one of the purest of the old Choctaw speech there is, because we haven't intermingled," Chief Smith says. "The language has bothered me for a long time. We need to address it."

Over the years the tribe has repeatedly attempted to teach the language to more of its members. A sixteen-week program led by Jackson is one of the latest efforts. The Tuesday night language classes at the tribal center have turned into more than he expected. "We talk a lot about some of the tribal history in our language classes," Jackson explains. "It's about the only avenue we have as to oral history. We talk openly about ourselves, the history of our own lives."

The down-to-earth former tribal chief says he learned something surprising in a recent class. "I brought up that my wife tells me I don't tell her I love her," he recalls. "In the eighteen or nineteen years I was home, I never saw my mom and dad hug each other or give each other a kiss good-bye. . . . Some young ladies in the class said it's still going on now. They told me, 'My husband tells me I don't tell him I love him enough.' This must be a tradition that we didn't know about, that Indian people never express what they think."

While some tribal members attend Jackson's language classes to renew their heritage, others take a more hands-on approach by reclaiming their tradition of basket making. Rose Fisher Blasingame, whose baskets are highly popular with collectors, is spearheading the renaissance of the craft within the tribe. She proudly traces the talent back to her great-great aunt Mary Lewis, the last of the tribe's basket makers. "The family was sharecroppers," Blasingame explains. "She'd take two baskets to a merchant, give one basket to him, and have him fill the other basket with seeds, sugar, flour, whatever she needed. I grew up hearing stories about how this lady helped her family."

Chief Smith says it's important to find the right people to learn. "It's got to be in a person's soul and heart to make a basket," she believes. She feels the tribe is fortunate to have a teacher who is young enough to teach the tribe for years to come.

In Blasingame's first class, twelve people eagerly penetrated the thickly wooded forest to learn the ancient craft. Once there, they chopped down ten canes each, then washed them in Trout Creek as their ancestors once did. At the tribal center, they arranged two long canes into predrilled tree stumps to help strip the bulk of the cane into sixty flexible pieces. They dyed the cane into several colors. A week later, class participants soaked up information on weaving the strips of cane into complexly designed baskets.

Gaining federal recognition has helped the tribe resurrect traditions like basket making and address educational, health, and housing issues. But unlike most other federally recognized tribes, the Jena band still had no land. "Without land, we couldn't create our own companies, our own jobs. We couldn't build schools to educate our kids and teach our language and culture," Clyde Jackson explains. "It's about economics, education, and tribal culture. You've got to have a foot to start with, then you can start doing some walking."

For the Jena band, the quest for land sometimes seemed as impossible as the five-month return to Oklahoma one hundred years ago. But by 2001 they had scraped together a total of sixty-two acres spread over two parishes in twelve separate locations. From these lands they hope to build their future. The Jena band formally asked the federal government to take the sixty-two acres into trust, allowing the land to be deemed a reservation.

Chief Smith explains that once the land is in trust, "you are a sovereign nation with your sovereign lands. With land comes lots of benefits, whether it's tax breaks or just the fact you're on your own land." Sovereignty means the tribe handles its own governance, including taxation, law enforcement, and social services. Without a reservation, the tribe has little jurisdiction. It also has no way to create jobs for its members as other tribes have done by building factories or gas stations.

While the three other federally recognized Louisiana tribes have introduced gaming to make substantial improvements, the Jena band's longtime lack of property has been a major stumbling block for economic development. When Smith first took office, she admits she "put gaming on the back burner." First, she insisted the tribe must help its members with the more immediate need of housing. "Our top priority is keeping people alive and healthy and in a standard home," she said then. The Jena band purchased houses for tribal members whose homes were in the worst condition and made numerous repairs to others. Then they returned to the issue of gaming.

"The Jena, we've had a long row to hoe all of our lives. We've never had anything. . . . How many more years can you wait and wait and your people are suffering?" Smith wonders. "We have to move forward and hope and pray that we make good decisions. We're still actively pursuing gaming."

Though the strength they draw from their culture has enabled them to overcome continued obstacles, the Jena band knows that compared to other tribes, they are among the poorest.

"They may have more dollars than we have, but we're far richer than they are," Chief Smith says, noting the Jena band has strong bloodlines and still practice many of their traditions. "What is worth the most? We're survivors. Whether we ever get a casino or allotment checks, we know who we are. We know where we came from, and we're gonna survive. We're just gonna do with what we have. We always have."

Held together by bootlaces, an old scrapbook preserves the portrait of Mary Jackson Jones. Taken at the Penick Indian School in the 1930s, the portrait recalls the brief time when the Jena band had its own school.

Abandoned long ago, the Whatley store still holds memories for Dorothy Smith (left), Milton Lewis, and Marie Kestner. Their father, Anderson Lewis, worked for many years as a sharecropper, obtaining supplies from the store. Smith remembers not being allowed into the front part of the store because she was Indian.

"WHETHER I'M NATIVE AMERICAN or black or white or Chinese or—like my daddy used to say, a Martian—I don't dwell on it. I'm thankful for what I get through the tribe, but didn't expect anything better or different. I think we're just all human, trying to be better than what we are. And that's hard to get to sometimes. I don't dwell on being Indian. I'm just one person. I don't think of it in a bad way or a good way—I'm just Dorothy."

"All of our Indian people lived around Trout Creek," explains elder Mary Jackson Jones. "It was a place where we used to hunt and fish, part of our original settlement area."

Morning light filters through pine trees to highlight the Whiterock Cemetery grave site of Choctaw Ziek Lewis. The World War II veteran died after returning from the war in 1946.

Tribal member Justin Jackson sweats through a day's work at the tribe's secluded cemetery. Maintaining Whiterock Cemetery has always been important to the tribe. Tribal elder Dorothy Lewis Smith remembers cleaning trips there when she was a child more than 40 years ago, when men did the heavy labor and women brought chicken and dumplings with cornbread.

Tribal member Larry Jackson says from the time he first played with toy trucks as a child, he knew he wanted to drive a truck for a living. He's been a truck driver since 1971. A Marine Corps veteran of the Vietnam War, Jackson helped administer the tribe's Title IV Indian education grant that funded an after-school tutoring program for children.

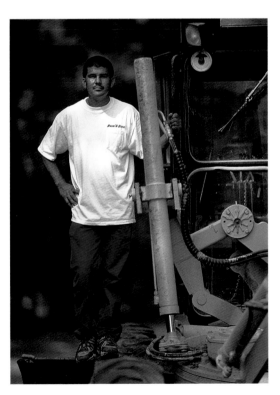

Hoping to stay close to home, tribal council member Chip Fisher holds on to a job driving a grader for a local trucking company. The tight job market in La Salle Parish, where high school graduates can only look to the unstable forestry and oil industries for work, forces many tribal members to move out of the area.

One of the tribe's first high school graduates, Clyde Jackson became tribal chief and later served as director of the Louisiana Office of Indian Affairs. As a Wildlife and Fisheries Department agent, he lives in the 60,000-acre Dewey W. Wills Wildlife Management Area.

Tribal member and LPN Darlene Lewis Billings checks the blood pressure of her sister, Dorothy Lewis Smith, during a home health visit. Grant money available since the tribe received federal recognition in 1995 has enabled tribal members to receive much-needed medical care and medicine through Indian Health Services.

One of the first priorities for the tribe after gaining federal recognition was to provide adequate housing for its members. Tribal elder Mary Jackson Jones, who helps care for her grandchildren (from left), Nathan Jones, Brittany Jackson, and Nick Jones, moved into this rented house after the floor of her previous home collapsed.

Elder Mary Jackson Jones crafts traditional chinaberry necklaces in her home. Jones is a highly respected source of tribal stories.

"*KWANOKA'SHA* IS SOMETHING that is spiritual. Daddy seen it and he described it to us. He threw Daddy a rock. He seen him just one time, and he brought the rock home. Daddy was sitting on the bank of the creek fishing, and the sun was just about going down. All the fish were gone. That rock fell just beside him. He knowed what it was. He looked up and there he seen it. About two feet tall, not quite that tall. When he looked up again it was already gone. . . . This spirit rock, it was given to you, and if you use it right you always will have that power. You always will help the people who need it."

Louisiana Army National Guard Major Cathy J. Vittoria, operations officer at the Gillis Long Center, respectfully welcomes Mary Jackson Jones to the Guard's facility for at-risk juveniles in Carville, the site of an old Indian village. An agreement with the federally recognized tribes requires the Guard to work with the tribes to protect traditional Native American cultural sites.

B. Cheryl Smith, chief of the Jena band, is one of only a handful of women who have been chosen to lead their tribes. "My tribe has been my life's career. Now is my chance to help our people get the things they need," says Smith.

Tribal council members (from left) Christine Norris, Chip Fisher, and Herman Jackson listen to a presentation by a Choctaw Christian group from Oklahoma during a council meeting in Jena. Elected according to the Jena Band of Choctaw constitution, the tribal council consists of four council members and a tribal chief.

Inside the Wigwam Food Court at the University of Louisiana at Monroe, tribal member Jennifer Jackson prepares for class. Jackson went on to become the first person in her family to earn a four-year degree.

"I WOULD SOMEDAY like for my children and niece and nephew to see where their family came from . . . to see how unique they and their family are. . . . Ultimately, I would hope for our future that we are able to someday have a reservation for our members to come back to and bring us together as a centralized tribe."

Jena band member Anna Barber (front) found many Choctaw friends, including (from left) Morgan Ben, Ira Ben, and Dyron Thompson, at Choctaw Central High School in Philadelphia, Mississippi. Barber says she would strongly encourage others to attend the school to learn more about their heritage: "When I first went to school [in Jena] I had some problems because I wasn't white enough, but when I went to Philadelphia I wasn't Indian enough. You know so much about both sides and you just have to know when to show some parts of it and when to show other parts of it. You learn to be a very well-rounded person. I think everybody should trace their background—everybody has a cultural tie to something, and you could learn so much about yourself."

Tribal member Ben Jackson lifts his Jena High School football helmet in tandem with his teammates before the start of a home football game. When tribal members first began attending public schools in the 1940s, athletics often helped them gain acceptance from their classmates.

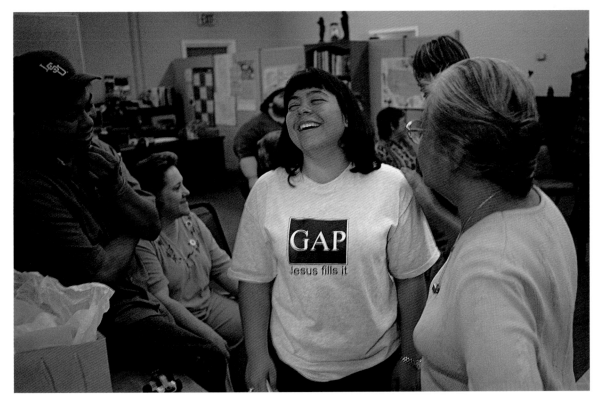

Placing an emphasis on education, tribal members celebrate the success of recent high school and college graduates. Sarah Jackson (center) graduated from Jena High School and plans to follow in the footsteps of Jennifer Jackson and attend the University of Louisiana at Monroe.

121

Tribal member Chip Fisher attempts to score during a basketball game at the tribe's annual Easter picnic. In times past, the Choctaw Indians were known for their enjoyment of stickball, or *ishtaboli*, which sometimes featured hundreds of players on each team.

Tribal member Wes Jackson dives for a ground ball during a softball tournament in Tullos, La. Besides hunting and fishing, softball is popular among tribal members.

Tribal member Clifton Jackson closes his eyes in prayer during an Easter sunrise service at the Temple Baptist Church in Jena.

"I ACCEPTED THE LORD when I was seven or eight years old; I don't see how a person could live without the Lord. He carried me through some good times and bad; everything I have I thank the Lord for. When I first got married, my job just opened up for me; the Lord took care of it and answered my prayers so my wife didn't have to work. I've got two good kids, maybe because of that. That's all blessings I've got from Him. Everything I have I credit Him for."

Tribal members enrolled in a basket making class travel to the waters of Trout Creek, much as their ancestors did before them. There they practice the traditional method of cleaning the cane used for making baskets. Jim Caldwell captured the cane cutting and cleaning for an U.S. Forest Service instructional and promotional video.

River cane cleaned in Trout Creek is stacked and ready for stripping.

Choctaw basket maker Rose Fisher Blasingame has revived her tribe's tradition of making cane baskets after a 40-year hiatus.

"WE NEED TO maintain our crafts, our traditions, our language. I learned from my grandparents about plants, making dyes and medicines and foods. . . . It's very important to me to keep us Choctaw, to make sure we always maintain what makes us different," explains Blasingame, who adds: "Being Choctaw is more than just making baskets. A lot of parts make up the whole. It's knowing I have an identity, that I belong."

The lid of one of Rose Fisher Blasingame's favorite baskets depicts the four directions of north, south, east, and west. She is reluctant to discuss the design's deeper meaning. "That goes back to the oral traditions from my grandparents. Some things are very important and will always be mine. The things that I keep within my family are not meant to be shared outside my culture," she explains.

Tribal member Rose Fisher Blasingame (right) teaches Mary Alice George how to split cane into flexible strips. Blasingame taught the class with the help of an economic recovery grant from the U.S. Forest Service.

Stretching a deer hide between two trees, tribal member Clyde Jackson begins the slow task of turning the hide into soft leather. Jackson learned to tan deer hides from his uncle, Anderson Lewis, and hopes to pass the knowledge to the next generation.

Tribal members Clara Henry (left) and Courtney Stapleton anticipate the start of the Choctaw Princess Pageant. The Jena Band of Choctaw princess is a visible representative of the tribe at community events, festivals, and pow wows.

Tribal member Theresa Stephens' son, Ian, pauses in his search for the last of the Easter eggs during the tribe's annual Easter picnic.

Tribal member Emily Stephens (left) and her friend Sara Holloway spend the day arm in arm during Howdy Neighbor Day celebrations in Jena's city park.

Tribal member Anna Barber spends time with Ira Ben, a Mississippi Choctaw tribal member. Barber's mother, Rose Fisher Blasingame, encouraged her to attend Choctaw Central High School in Philadelphia, Mississippi, to expose her to the tradition and culture of the Mississippi Choctaw and perhaps to bring home a Choctaw son-in-law.

Before leaving for marine boot camp, Lawrence Chapman (lower left) watches his brother Lester Chapman leap into Trout Creek at a local swimming hole known as Buttermilk. According to tribal elders an old woman who sold milk would store buttermilk in the cool waters of the creek.

Tribal members Candess and Lester Chapman ride home in their brother Lawrence's pickup truck after enjoying their last sibling swim before Lawrence left for boot camp.

On a quest for land to call their own, more than 50 tribal members and spouses gather to inspect a proposed land site near Trout, La. The tribe eventually built a new multipurpose center at another location nearby.

Time Line

4000 B.C. Chitimacha exist at their present location in the lower Mississippi River delta.

1700–700 B.C. Poverty Point inhabitants in northeastern Louisiana build complex ridged earthworks and mounds overlooking the Mississippi River floodplain.

A.D. 1540 Spanish explorers led by de Soto encounter the Coushatta and raid a village near the Tennessee River, kidnapping the chief and other leaders.

1541 De Soto discovers the Mississippi River near the town of Quizquiz, where he first encounters the powerful ancestors of the Tunica. The Quizquiz were mound builders and great warriors.

1699 The French find the remnants of the Quizquiz on the lower Yazoo River. By this time they are called the Tunica.

1706–1731 The Tunica occupy the area around modern-day Angola, Louisiana.

1706–1718 The French go to war with the Chitimacha for 12 years.

1729–1730 The Tunica ally with the French against the Natchez, leading to the defeat of the Natchez tribe and the scattering of its survivors.

1731–1763 The Tunica inhabit the Trudeau area, where they bury the famed Tunica Treasure.

1783 The Treaty of Paris ends the American Revolution, and the Coushatta and other Creek tribes living in the state of Georgia fear retaliation for siding with the British. Anti-British Creek factions surrender 800 square miles of territory to Georgia, igniting bitter arguments among the tribes.

1786 The Creeks declare war on Georgia, seeking to recover ceded territories.

1790 The Tunica-Biloxi tribe relocates to modern-day Avoyelles Parish, settling on the 132 acres that was all that remained of a Spanish land grant of three square leagues.

1790 Fearing a general Indian war, President George Washington asks Congress to sign the Treaty of New York between the U.S. and the Creek tribes. This agreement spurs Spain to make new alliances with the Indians in their territories.

1793 The Treaty of San Lorenzo establishes the 31st parallel as the boundary between the U.S. and Spain. The Alabama Coushatta begin migrating westward into friendlier Spanish territory.

1803 With the Louisiana Purchase, the U.S. extends the sovereign protection afforded the Chitimacha by the French and Spanish governments.

1812 Many Coushatta settle in a neutral area west of Natchitoches between the disputed borders of the U.S. and Spain.

1812 The War of 1812 causes major divisions among native tribes, some of whom help the fledgling U.S., while others support the British. Indian allies of the British will be severely punished by the U.S. after the war ends.

1813 The Creek Civil War splits the Creek Confederacy. The Coushatta participate, losing warriors and land.

1814 Andrew Jackson crushes the Creek Civil War, killing 3,000 Indians and seizing 22 million acres of Creek land as the price for peace.

1819 Spain and the U.S. agree to a common border on the Trinity River. Large numbers of Alabama-Coushatta continue moving west to escape encroaching American settlers.

1824 The Bureau of Indian Affairs is established within the War Department.

1830 Congress passes the Removal Act, immediately followed by the Treaty of Dancing Rabbit Creek with the Choctaw, which forces tribes east of the Mississippi River to relocate to west of the Mississippi River. Most go to the Oklahoma territory, but one group of Choctaw settles near Jena, Louisiana.

1831 The U.S. Supreme Court recognizes native tribes as "domestic dependent nations." In an 1812 decision, the Court had declared that such nations had a right to self-government.

1848 U.S. District Court confirms Chitimacha title to 1,093 acres of land in St. Mary Parish.

1850 Coushatta in Louisiana establish a village on the Calcasieu River near Kinder.

1854 Encroaching homesteaders prompt many Coushatta to move to land purchased near Elton.

1871 Congress prohibits the making of further treaties with native tribes.

1887 The Dawes Severalty Act, or General Allotment Act, allots parcels of reservation lands to tribal members and sells off remaining acreage, depriving native people of more than 90 million acres, or 2/3 of their land.

1898 The U.S. government places 160 acres in trust for the Coushatta tribe.

1906–1911 Twenty-one Chitimacha students ranging from 11 to 25 years of age are sent to Carlisle Indian School in Carlisle, Pennsylvania.

1919 The U.S. government formally recognizes the Chitimacha Tribe of Louisiana as a sovereign nation, establishing a 261-acre reservation with land repurchased for the tribe.

1924 The Snyder Act makes Native Americans citizens of the United States. Many had given their lives for the country in World War I without being regarded as citizens.

1930 The Bureau of Indian Affairs assumes responsibility for the Coushatta tribe's education.

1932 The Penick School opens in Eden to educate children of the Jena Band of Choctaw.

1934 The Chitimacha tribe secures its first school, a condemned black school building.

1934 The Wheeler-Howard Indian Reorganization Act ends land allotments and provides for restoration of tribal power and culture.

1953 The Bureau of Indian Affairs ends its trusteeship and discontinues services to the Coushatta tribe.

1970 The Chitimacha Tribe of Louisiana adopts its own tribal constitution.

1971 The Department of the Interior approves the Chitimacha constitution, and the tribe receives federal recognition.

1973   The Coushatta tribe wins restoration of BIA services.

1975   Federal proclamation reserves 15 acres as Coushatta Indian reservation land.

1976   Chief Joseph Alcide Pierite, the last chief of the Tunica, dies. This chieftainship extended in an unbroken line back to at least the 17th century and perhaps even to the Quizquiz.

1978   The Chitimacha tribe opens the Chitimacha Tribal School. Earl Barbry, Sr., begins his first term as chairman of the Tunica-Biloxi tribe.

1981   The Tunica-Biloxi tribe receives federal recognition.

1988   The Indian Gaming Regulatory Act provides for federal regulation of gaming by Indian tribes after court cases determine states do not have regulatory power over tribes.

1990   Congress enacts the Native American Graves Protection and Repatriation Act, providing for the protection of Native American burial sites and the return of human remains and artifacts to federally recognized tribes.

1993   The Chitimacha tribe opens Cypress Bayou Casino, expanding earlier bingo operations.

1994   The Tunica-Biloxi tribe opens Grand Casino Avoyelles, later renamed Paragon Casino Resort.

1995   The Coushatta tribe opens Grand Casino Coushatta.

1995   The Jena Band of Choctaw Indians receives federal recognition.